PRACTICING LAW WITH[out] CLIENTS

Making a Living as a Freelance Lawyer

by David A. Robinson

ABA American Bar Association • Section of Law Practice Management

To My Parents,
Anne S. and Jack Z. Robinson

Cover design by Gini Kondziolka

Printed in the United States of America.

Library of Congress Catalog Card Number 96-86562
ISBN 1-57073-403-8

00 99 98 97 96 5 4 3 2 1

CONTENTS

Appendix A

Appendix B

ABOUT THE AUTHOR

David A. Robinson is a sole practitioner in Springfield, Massachusetts, specializing in labor and employment law. He has some clients of his own, but he devotes most of his time to helping other lawyers represent their own clients in labor and employment cases. He is their legal researcher, writer, and strategic consultant.

A native of Springfield, he received his B.A. in 1974 from George Washington University and his J.D. in 1977 from Washington University in St. Louis, where he was senior editor of the law review. He taught legal ethics at Western New England College School of Law from 1979 to 1982 and was a legal and political correspondent for WWLP-TV in Springfield in 1987–88.

He is a member of the ABA Section of Law Practice Management and Section of Labor and Employment Law and the Massachusetts Bar Association Section of Labor and Employment and Section of Small Firm Management.

ACKNOWLEDGMENTS

I owe an enormous debt of gratitude to virtually the entire legal community of Springfield, Massachusetts. Springfield lawyers have provided me with the opportunities and experiences upon which this book is based. Space does not permit me to name them all, but I will name the ones who have helped me the most: Vincent A. Bongiorni (and his legal assistant, Kay Burkott), Roberta L. Brundrett, John C. Bryson, David and Merwyn Burstein, Owen S. Clark, Bruce E. Colton, Judith A. Cross, Gerard J. DiSanti, Charles J. Emma, Neil Fieldman, Richard M. Gaberman, Perman Glenn III, Dean E. Goldblatt, Alan R. Goodman, Efrem A. Gordon, Robert A. Gordon, Edward N. Hurley, Mary E. Hurley-Marks, Richard J. Ianello, Warren J. Jacks Jr. (and his legal assistant, Carolyn Letendre), Christopher Johnson, Daniel M. Kelly, Thomas A. Kenefick, Stanley D. Komack, Thomas S. Locke, Arthur M. Marshall, Patricia and Thomas Martinelli, John and Mary McNally, Jay and Leonard Michelman, John E. Miller, Joseph P. Minardi, Cornelius W. Phillips III, Harold and Steven Resnic, Robert M. Rosen, John D. Ross III, Jack F. St. Clair, Burton A. Shaker, John C. Sikorski, Susan E. Silver, Alan D. Sisitsky, Peter Slepchuk Jr., Kimberly Sudnick, Frederick M. Sullivan, John and Linda Thompson, Seymour Tillman, and Patricia A. Zak.

I thank the following Boston lawyers for providing me with speaking and writing opportunities: John B. Cochran, George P. Field, Sarah Garraty, Robert B. Gordon, Vivian Hsu, Nancy D. Israel, Ellen J. Messing, Gary J. Oberstein, Douglas T. Schwarz, and Ilene Robinson Sunshine.

I thank the following lawyers for submitting ideas and offering assistance with the book: Laurel H. Brandt and Louis S. Robin of Longmeadow, Massachusetts; Robert T. Gill of Boston, Richard B. Schafer of Natick, Massachusetts; David L. Forsyth and Donna M.

Killoughey of Tempe, Arizona; Kenneth Landau of Mineola, New York; Gary Munneke of New York; Kathryn S. Marshall of Anacortes, Washington; and Roger E. Schechter of Washington, D.C.

I thank the *Massachusetts Lawyers Weekly* and the Hampden County, Boston, and Massachusetts bar associations for helping me spread the good news about wholesale law practice.

I thank the Hampden County, Western New England, and University of Connecticut law libraries, the Springfield City Library, and the Storrs Library in Longmeadow, Massachusetts, for their research facilities and friendly service.

I thank the ABA (particularly Executive Editor Beverly Loder in Chicago and project manager Professor Bill Henslee from Pepperdine University School of Law in California) for publishing the book.

I thank the following individuals and organizations for their assistance during 1986–91, when I tried to quit law practice and change careers entirely: WWLP-TV (particularly Lynn Barry, Bill Pepin, and Keith Silver) in Springfield, Massachusetts; Aetna Life & Casualty Company; lawyers Catherine P. Kligerman and Paul N. Shapera of Hartford, Connecticut; and Bart Tessler of the Mutual/NBC Radio Network.

I thank my law school alma mater, Washington University in St. Louis.

Last, and most, I thank my parents, Anne and Jack Robinson, and the rest of my family for their unwavering support throughout my life and career.

FOREWORD

In recent years, increasing numbers of lawyers have become dissatisfied with the traditional practice of law in firms, corporate legal departments, and government agencies. They have left these settings for nonlegal positions, often for less-adversarial work. Bar associations and even the popular press are publishing articles bemoaning the loss of civility in legal practice and "burnout" among lawyers.

The ABA Section of Law Practice Management, through its publishing arm, LPM Publishing, has assisted lawyers in making career choices through such books as *Changing Jobs: A Handbook for Lawyers for the 1990s,* edited by Heidi L. McNeil, and *Breaking Traditions: Work Alternatives for Lawyers,* edited by Donna M. Killoughey. We are pleased to add David Robinson's *Practicing Law Without Clients* to this line.

Mr. Robinson sets forth his blueprint for practicing "wholesale" law by engagingly relating the successes and pitfalls he encountered in developing his own practice as a freelance legal researcher/writer/consultant. He describes the steps for setting up your own such practice, or for determining whether and how to engage the services of your own legal research consultant.

If you do not want to represent clients directly and are dissatisfied with the adversarial nature of law practice, if you want to hang out your shingle as a "legal writer" rather than a "legal fighter," Mr. Robinson gives you the tools to succeed, as well as the confidence that your choice will lead to a personally and professionally rewarding career.

This book defines the wholesale law practice; helps you decide if wholesale law is a career option for you; explains how the use of freelance writing consultants can improve the "retail" lawyer's practice; shows how to obtain engagements by large and small firms and corporate legal departments; discusses ethical considerations; and details the steps for starting, managing, and marketing a wholesale law practice. Mr Robinson argues persuasively for development of a sector of wholesale lawyering and suggests ways to start organized support groups to assist such practitioners.

LPM Publishing is committed to assisting lawyers to obtain greater satisfaction in their careers. We are excited about Mr. Robinson's approach and trust you will find this book to be stimulating and motivating.

Robert J. Conroy
Judith L. Grubner
Co-Chairs
LPM Publishing

OVERVIEW

The Freelance Lawyer: A "Wholesale" Lawyer Working for "Retail" Lawyers

This book explains how lawyers who enjoy legal research and writing more than they enjoy client contact and adversarial struggle can earn a living by becoming freelance legal researchers and writers for the lawyers who do enjoy client contact and adversarial struggle but do not enjoy legal research and writing.

The book will refer to these freelance lawyers as *wholesale lawyers* because they would be working mainly for other lawyers rather than directly for clients and would be independent contractors rather than employees of these other lawyers. The services they will provide—legal research, legal writing, and strategic legal advice—will be called *wholesale legal services*. The lawyers to whom they provide these services will be called *retail lawyers*. Retail lawyers represent clients directly and battle with adversaries directly. Nearly all practicing lawyers are retail lawyers. Some lawyers are both: they represent clients and battle with adversaries directly, and they also provide wholesale legal services to other retail lawyers.

The book also explains how if enough lawyers were to switch from retail to wholesale law practice, it might help alleviate some of the major problems facing lawyers today: career dissatisfaction, the lawyer "glut," the financial plight of the average sole practitioner, the inability of low-income Americans to afford legal counsel, and the lack of "quiet time" for lawyers to concentrate on complex research and writing tasks.

Primarily, however, the book focuses on the thousands of lawyers in this country who enjoy law intellectually but do not enjoy the *practice* of law. They enjoy legal research, legal writing, and collegial legal discussions with other lawyers, but they do not enjoy the "retail" functions of law practice: the difficult clients, the constant clashes with adversaries, and the pressure to bring in more clients. They do not enjoy being on the front lines of the legal battlefield. They prefer legal *writing* to legal *fighting*. This book explains how such lawyers can earn a living with their intellectual legal talents rather than their "retail" talents.

The legal profession as a whole has never had a separate wholesale sector, i.e., a sector of lawyers who mainly do legal research, writing, and consulting for other lawyers. Large and medium-sized law firms have a wholesale sector (associates) and a retail sector (partners), although, to be sure, many large and medium-sized firm partners do their own legal research and writing and many of their associates also perform retail functions. But solo lawyers and small-firm lawyers who lack associates usually have to do their own legal research and writing.

This book proposes the creation of a wholesale sector within the legal profession to assist those lawyers who do not have associates to do their wholesale chores for them. It would be an informal, unofficial sector. Any lawyer could join it, any lawyer could use it, any lawyer could ignore it completely, and any lawyer could work in both the retail and wholesale sectors simultaneously, i.e., maintain a retail law practice and also provide wholesale legal services to other lawyers. The sectors would be functional rather than formal, just as industries are functionally organized into retail and wholesale sectors without any formal or legal division between the two. The division in the legal profession would be nearly invisible. Lawyers would not have to declare themselves "retail lawyers" or "wholesale lawyers" on their bar registration cards, office signs, Yellow Pages listings, letterheads, or anywhere else.

But creating a wholesale *sector* of lawyers is not your immediate concern. Your immediate concern is how *you* can become a full-time or part-time wholesale lawyer—a freelance legal researcher, writer, and consultant for other lawyers. You do not need a "sector" to do this—you can do it on your own. This book will show you how. It will also show you how lawyers who enjoy retail law practice can improve their practices by using the services of wholesale lawyers.

The concept of wholesale lawyering is not entirely new. There have always been wholesale lawyers here and there. They have been called contract lawyers, per-diem lawyers, independent contractor counsel, consulting lawyers, project-specific of counsel, and, over the last year or two, virtual associates. This book does not invent the concept of wholesale lawyering any more than Henry Ford invented the automobile. What Ford invented was the mass production of the automobile. This book tries to do for wholesale legal services what Ford did for automobiles: make them available and affordable to all who need them and make them a livelihood for the thousands of people who produce them.

Wholesale benefits

How would this ease the problems mentioned earlier? It would improve lawyer morale, because lawyers who prefer the wholesale functions to the retail functions could spend most or all of their time on the wholesale functions, and lawyers who prefer the retail functions could concentrate more on the retail functions.

It would reduce the lawyer "glut" in two ways. First, many lawyers would wholly or partially drop out of retail law practice and would no longer be competing with retail lawyers for clients. Second, many lawyers who want to leave the legal profession entirely and embark on new careers would be better situated to do so. They could first become wholesale lawyers, which would free them from the tug of clients and long-term obligations. This would enable them to look more easily for work outside the legal profession and earn a living in the meantime. They could also moonlight as wholesale lawyers if they need extra income after they land new careers.

It would enhance the incomes of lawyers who are more scholarly than they are street-smart, and of lawyers who want to expand their retail law practices but are too bogged down now with legal research and writing.

It would provide as good, if not better, a living as the average sole practitioner earns.

It would improve client service, because legal documents

would be written by top-notch, specialized legal writers who have whole mornings, whole days, and even whole weeks to set aside for complex research and writing, without being constantly interrupted by phone calls and other distractions.

It would improve the delivery of legal services to low-income Americans, because wholesale lawyers, who have very low overhead, might be willing on occasion to provide, at low hourly rates, some retail legal services to low-income people who cannot afford standard, retail legal fees.

This book, however, is intended to benefit *you,* the individual lawyer. If it also benefits the legal profession as a whole, all the better.

Who's "wholesale"?

As mentioned before, wholesale lawyers are sometimes called contract lawyers. Generally speaking the terms "wholesale lawyer" and "contract lawyer" have the same meaning. I prefer the term "wholesale lawyer" because it truly captures the essence of what freelance legal researchers/writers/consultants do. They sell their services to "retail" lawyers, who in turn use these services for the benefit of the ultimate consumer—the client.

A wholesale lawyer is *not* the same as a "temporary lawyer." The term "temporary lawyer" usually means a lawyer who is employed by an employment agency that furnishes law firms and corporate legal departments with lawyers on a temporary or project basis.[1] The temp usually works normal business hours, on site (at the law firm or corporation), and for only one law firm or corporation at a time. The law firm or corporation pays the employment agency an hourly fee (depending on the agency and the particular temp, the range is approximately $40–$150 an hour)[2] out of which the agency pays the temp. The temp does not receive a percentage of the fee that the law firm receives from the clients whose cases the temp handles.

A "wholesale lawyer," on the other hand, is self-employed, does not work for an agency, and works on many cases for several or many different lawyers concurrently. Wholesale lawyers market themselves directly to these lawyers, rather than relying on an agency to find work for them. These lawyers pay the wholesale lawyer an hourly fee (usually ranging from $25 to $50 an hour), a fixed fee (say, $900 to research, write, and gather supporting materials for a motion for summary judgment), or a contingent fee (say, one-third of the fee the retail lawyer receives from the client), or a combination hourly/contingent fee (say, $20 per hour plus 20 percent of the lawyer's fee). Wholesale lawyers have offices of their own (an office at home will do, but there are advantages to having an office in the immediate vicinity of other lawyers; see Chapter 4) and work whenever and wherever it is mutually convenient to them and the retail lawyer.

Temps work and get paid only when the temp agency is able to place them in assignments. Although there are thousands of lawyers seeking work through temp agencies, the number who actually get placed is unclear. According to the *Legal Recruiters 1996 Directory,* an *American Lawyer* supplement compiled by surveying the membership of the National Association of Legal Search Consultants, 201 of the 253 members declined to disclose the number of placements they made.[3] One leading agency, Special Counsel International, receives 225 applications for every position it can fill[4] and, according to its ad, places only lawyers with "top 10 law school credentials, or top 5 percent class standing."[5] A partner at a major New York law firm says, "For a temporary position I can call a good agency and invariably receive a stack of resumes of lawyers overqualified for the position."[6] Thus, many temps work infrequently or not at all.

Furthermore, most temporary lawyer agencies cater to large and medium-sized law firms and in-house corporate legal departments,[7] who can afford to pay the agencies' fees. That means, first, that opportunities for temporary lawyers exist mainly in large cities, not medium-sized and smaller cities and towns. Second, because large and medium-sized law firms and corporate legal departments usually prefer to hire temps who have worked in large or medium-sized law firms or corporate legal departments themselves, lawyers who have never worked in those situations have little chance of landing such assignments.

If you are considering temping for a living, you should talk not only to the temp agencies but also to the temps themselves. Try to ascertain how often they work. Try to get some type of assurance from the agency that you will work often, or at least ask the agency if it is okay for you to do some wholesale lawyering—for lawyers you found on your own—while you are between assignments. Temping is great work—if you can get it.

Personal concerns

If you are contemplating becoming a wholesale lawyer, especially a full-time wholesale lawyer (working almost exclusively for other lawyers and having few or no clients of your own), you probably have some concerns that are more profound than simply how to start, manage, market, and earn a living at it. You have personal and psychological concerns.

- How will your transition from retail to wholesale law practice affect your career in the long run?
- Will your fellow lawyers, retail clients, family, and friends regard you as a failure or a quitter for switching from the high-powered world of retail law practice to the pastoral world of wholesale law practice?
- Will you make less money than if you stayed in full-time retail law practice?
- If you were to stay in full-time retail law practice and work hard, wouldn't you eventually attract better clients and better cases, make more money, perhaps land a job in a big law firm, and in any event be happier than you are now? And if so, why give up retail law practice for wholesale law practice?
- As a wholesale lawyer, will you spend the rest of your career in obscurity, laboring in the shadows of the retail lawyers you serve?
- If you don't like wholesale law practice, can you easily switch back to retail law practice?
- Because you are dissatisfied with law practice, wouldn't you be better off quitting law altogether and finding another career rather than simply switching from retail to wholesale law practice?

I faced all these quandaries myself as I traveled the road from retail to wholesale law practice. It was a long and winding road for me, but having traveled it, I can now draw you a map that will make the road smoother and faster for you. The map illustrates the potholes, sharp curves, exits to nowhere, and comfort stations along the way. Many of you reading this book probably have law school credentials and law practice experiences similar to mine, so the early stretches of road will look familiar to you. When the road becomes unfamiliar, the map will show you what to watch out for. It will guide you through the quandaries. The rest of this overview is that road map.

The road to wholesale law practice

The road began for me in 1977, when I graduated in the middle of my class from Washington University Law School in St. Louis, a good, but nonelite law school. I made law review through a writing competition, not grades. I returned to my hometown of Springfield, Massachusetts, passed the bar, and was rejected by all of the larger Springfield law firms with whom I sought employment.

I was offered, and I accepted, what is probably the most typical job for a new lawyer: working as an associate of a sole practitioner who handles mostly plaintiffs' personal injury cases, divorce cases, misdemeanors, collections, and residential real estate closings, and represents some small businesses. My salary was $125 a week plus 60 percent of the fees I brought in (I didn't bring in much). I learned about many areas of the law, and I enjoyed the research and writing assignments I was given, but I found most of the work to be distasteful.

I quit after two years and opened my own solo practice. Nothing improved. I thought many of my clients were obnoxious, their causes petty, and their demands unreasonable. Many were oblivious to their own wrongdoing and to whatever merits the other side had. I often doubted whether my clients were telling me the truth. I hated when a client would ask me to write a nasty letter to someone or to sue someone when I was not even sure whether my client was telling the truth.

I hated negotiating with opposing counsel. I felt (and still feel) that negotiation on a client's behalf is basically a bluff in which one lawyer makes a demand that he knows is far more than his client is willing to accept and the other lawyer makes an offer that she knows is far less than her client is willing to pay. Honesty (i.e., declaring what your client really thinks) is self-defeating. While teaching legal ethics at Western New England College School of Law in 1980, I came across an article in the *American Bar Foundation Research Journal* by Professor James J. White (author of a UCC hornbook) entitled "Machiavelli and the Bar: Ethical Limitations on Lying in Negotiation." White observed, "To conceal one's true position, to mislead an opponent about one's true settling point, is the essence of negotiation."[8] That quote haunted me then and haunts me now.

I dabbled in some less adversarial, transactional legal matters, but found them to be either boring or simply too difficult to learn on my own (one frustrating aspect of solo practice is that you often have no one to teach you how to do things).

I was always struggling to get paid. I listened to endless sob stories from my clients about how little money they had to pay me. And being the soft-hearted person that I am, I hated asking for the money anyway. I often accepted far less than I thought my services were worth. As a result, my total income during my first seven years of practice (1977–84) was about the same as it would have been had I been a high school teacher.

My income improved with the booming Massachusetts economy of 1985–86, but I still hated the work. I was despondent. I thought I might be happier in a law firm, and I did make a few attempts to join medium-sized firms and in-house corporate legal departments, but they rejected me. A partner (and friend of mine) in a twenty-five-lawyer firm politely explained to me that, with rare exceptions, large and medium-sized firms and in-house legal departments hire only three types of lawyers: (1) lawyers fresh out of law school; (2) lawyers from other large or medium-sized law firms or in-house corporate legal departments; and (3) government lawyers, such as judicial clerks, prosecutors, judges, legislators, and lawyers from federal, state, and municipal agencies; they do not hire sole practitioners. I thought he was just making this up so that I would not take the rejection personally. But I conducted a little study of my own and determined that he was telling the truth. I looked at the names on the letterheads of all the major Springfield law firms and thought about where all those lawyers were when they joined those firms (I knew most of these lawyers personally, so I knew their career paths). Hardly any had come from solo or small-firm practice. I read a famous 1982 study, *Chicago Lawyers: The Social Structure of the Bar,* which found that only 9 percent of lawyers who began in firms with fewer than ten lawyers ever moved to firms of ten or more lawyers, and of lawyers with less than twenty years of experience, the figure was only 6.5 percent.[9] I noticed in the "lateral hires" section of the *National Law Journal* that virtually all the laterals had moved from one large or medium-sized firm or in-house legal department to another. The same was true of nearly all the lawyers in the *Directory of Corporate Counsel,* which lists in-house lawyers. I concluded that a lawyer in solo or small-firm (five or fewer lawyers) practice had little chance of being hired by a large or medium-sized law firm or corporate legal department.

My purpose in mentioning this is not to criticize the law firms and corporate legal departments. Virtually every lawyer I know in these firms and departments is very bright, capable, hard-working, honest, and achieved better law school grades than I did. Perhaps half of them went to higher-ranked law schools than I did. Had I less respect for them, I would not have tried so hard to join them. My purpose is rather to point out that if you are a solo or small-firm lawyer and are dissatisfied with law practice, your strategy should not be to hope that a large or medium-sized law firm or in-house legal department will someday hire you. It could happen, but your chances are slim.

The road not taken

By March 1986, I was fed up with solo law practice and had given up trying to land a job with a large firm or in-house legal department. I decided to quit law altogether and pursue "the road not taken"—the career I had always dreamed about and had seriously considered when I graduated from college in 1974 but abandoned when I went to law school instead: broadcast journalism. I took some broadcasting courses, called some friends in the local TV industry, and after much effort landed a job as a part-time reporter at WWLP-TV (an NBC affiliate) in Springfield in January 1987.

I loved TV reporting. I had many exciting experiences, covered many fascinating trials (I was the legal correspondent and also covered political stories) and interviewed many famous people including George Bush, Bob Dole, Elizabeth Dole, Ted Kennedy, Michael Dukakis, and Tom Brokaw. Unfortunately, TV reporters in small markets such as Springfield make peanuts—less than $25,000 a year. TV *anchors* earn more, but there were no anchor positions available locally. Each month, I had to dig into my savings to make ends meet.

I could not work full-time at WWLP because—and this is very important for any sole practitioner who is contemplating quitting law practice to consider—I was still spending about twenty hours a week trying to wrap up my law practice. In addition to being a pain in my neck, my law practice had become a ball and chain around my foot. As I painfully learned, it is difficult for a small-firm lawyer (especially a sole practitioner) with a busy practice (like many of you, I did not make much money but I was always busy) to simply walk away from that practice, even if he or she definitely wants to and already has another career in mind. There are practical, ethical, and financial obstacles. A small-firm lawyer might have dozens of open files, including cases being handled on a contingent-fee basis, which usually means the lawyer is ethically and contractually bound to pursue these cases to completion, regardless of how many years that takes. Even though I decided to give up law in 1986, it took me until early 1988 to finally wrap up my cases even though I had managed to withdraw from many cases and refer them to other lawyers. Of course, referring good cases to other lawyers is easy; referring the "dogs" is more difficult. This process was unsettling to many of my clients—which weighed on my conscience—but I was unwilling to sacrifice my entire career just to keep a few clients happy.

Worse yet, while the solo is trying to close down his practice, he is not taking on any new clients. So his income diminishes rapidly. And what if his new career doesn't work out? Can he call back the clients he shuffled off to other lawyers and ask for a second chance? Can he call other lawyers and ask them for a job? If he does, he had better be prepared for rejection.

Converting from a retail to a wholesale law practice, on the other hand, is easier to reverse if it does not work out. It is a very subtle change. The wholesale lawyer is listed in the Yellow Pages with the other lawyers, has an office and every other outward appearance of being a retail lawyer, and is always free to accept retail clients. Wholesale law practice is also easier to walk away from, or at least curtail, if another career opportunity—including a nonlegal career opportunity of interest—comes up. The wholesale lawyer has few or no commitments to clients, mostly short-term commitments to lawyers, and a few long-term commitments to lawyers that can probably be honored even while pursuing a nonlegal career.

Although I was reluctant to leave Springfield, I made a halfhearted effort to advance to a bigger TV market such as Boston or New York. But TV news jobs in big cities are extremely difficult to land; there are thousands of reporters competing for a few dozen jobs. So after two exhilarating but destitute years on the air, I quit WWLP in late 1988 (after the presidential election), and tried to land a decent-paying job entirely outside the legal profession.

This turned out to be the most humiliating experience of my life. Potential employers would ask me: "What's the matter, couldn't you make a living as a lawyer or TV celebrity?" "Gee, all the lawyers I know are rich; what's wrong with you?" "What do you mean you don't like practicing law? It's a lot more exciting than working here. I've got two kids in law school myself. They're gonna make a bundle." "What happened, did you have a nervous breakdown or get disbarred?" I swear to you, I was asked every one of these humiliating questions during the winter of 1988–89.

I applied for editorial, marketing, publishing, and public relations jobs, mostly with educational and nonprofit organizations. I thought my TV and legal backgrounds would help me, but I was wrong. I received no offers. I thought I might enjoy being a high school social studies teacher, so I enrolled in a teacher certification course at a local college. I figured I would have an edge by reason of having taught law school part-time for three years. No one was impressed. I was told that I needed either 180 or 300 (I forget which) hours of unpaid student teaching at the secondary school level and that, by the way, there were no job openings in social studies anyway. I applied for social studies openings at inner-city private and parochial schools (which did not require certification) in Hartford, Connecticut, twenty-five miles to the south. No takers. I applied for teaching jobs at various local colleges, but they told me that the only courses I was qualified to teach (besides law school courses) were business law and criminal justice, and that there were no full-time openings. Full-time teaching positions at law schools are extremely difficult to land, so I did not even try. I was turned down for administrative jobs at the colleges and at other nonprofit organizations. Some told me that I was unqualified, some told me I was overqualified, most gave me no reason at all, and some did not even reply.

However—and here is yet another obstacle facing the small-firm lawyer who wants to leave law entirely—I think there is an additional reason they rejected me, even though no one told me this. Except for my boss at the TV station, where I was a part-time employee working a rather eclectic job that had little if anything to do with the work I was now applying for, I did not have a "direct supervisor" to recommend me to prospective employers. I had been a *self-employed* lawyer for the past ten years. Even though I listed my TV boss and some prominent lawyers and nonlawyers as references, there was still no one who could attest to my being a good, full-time employee in a normal job.

But even if a small-firm (or, for that matter, large-firm) lawyer does have a direct supervisor, the reference issue is still problematic. Lawyers who want to leave law might be reluctant to tell their supervisors that they are looking for work outside the legal profession. Supervisors would then know that the lawyers are dissatisfied with law and might fire them, regardless of whether they have found another job.

By December 1988, I was broke. I did some substitute teaching for $50 a day and loaded boxes for a trucking company for $9 an hour a few hours a day, but I needed a steady job—any steady job—immediately, just to survive while I continued to search for an adequate nonlegal job.

Totally desperate, I looked at the Hartford help-wanted ads (I was tired of the humiliation of being rejected in and near Springfield, where I was a well-known lawyer/journalist) and saw a job opening for which I was exceptionally well-qualified. It was in a profession I hated but knew rather well. I couldn't be fussy anymore, so I called the number and was invited for an interview. The job paid $450 a week (which I could live on for a while) and was short-term, so the employer would not mind my continuing to look for other jobs while working there. The job: legal secretary.

Not surprisingly, the first question I was asked at the interview was why I wanted to be a legal secretary. I was, after all, a real lawyer. I responded that I did not enjoy practicing law, that I had just left a TV job, that I was taking evening courses towards my teacher certification, and that I needed a short-term, 9-to-5 job to make ends meet until I got certified and found a teaching job. I was hired.

So there I was, thirty-six years old, a lawyer with thirty-five jury trials under my belt, nine appellate cases reported in the N.E.2d (mostly criminal cases), a law review alumnus of the thirty-first best law school in the country (according to the 1996 *U.S. News & World Report* rankings), three years as an adjunct faculty member at Western New England College School of Law, and two years as a TV reporter during which I interviewed major national figures, working as a legal *secretary?!*

Back on track

But were it not for that job, this book would not have been written. That job was the seed that eventually sprouted into my wholesale law practice. Although I was overqualified and found much of the work boring, I enjoyed working in a law office in which I was not directly responsible for the clients. And while $450 a week isn't great, at least I didn't have to scratch and scrape to receive it. I only had to show up and do my job as best I could. I even got to do a little legal research and writing (even in my darkest days as a retail lawyer, I always enjoyed legal research and writing). But I still kept looking for jobs outside the legal profession. Four months later, not having found such a job, I took a higher-paying job as a paralegal for a plaintiffs' personal injury lawyer. Again I enjoyed the atmosphere and whatever legal research and writing was assigned to me, but I continued to look for jobs outside the legal profession.

In December 1989 I saw an article in *Time* that took some of the sting out of the rejection I was getting from nonlegal employers. The article was about lawyers leaving the legal profession.[10] I expected to read about lawyers getting jobs as managers, marketers, and other traditional, nonlegal jobs. But to my surprise, these lawyers were not getting traditional jobs. They were not being paid salaries or wages. They had either started ventures of their own or were selling products on commission. I looked further into this by reading a book cited in the article *Running From the Law: Why Good Lawyers Are Getting Out of the Legal Profession,* by legal-career advisor Deborah Arron. Once again, nearly all the lawyers mentioned started their own ventures after leaving law. They were not hired by anyone and were not receiving a salary. They were self-employed. I empathized with these lawyers because undoubtedly many of them had applied for regular jobs but were rejected as I was. Although some probably started their own ventures because they wanted to and had the money to, others did so by default.

In any event, I no longer took the rejection personally. I realized that, for whatever reason, experienced lawyers have difficulty getting hired for nonlegal jobs. Ironically, it might be easier for lawyers fresh out of law school to land such jobs, for they do not have as much explaining to do.

I also conducted my own little study. I made a list of lawyers I knew who had left law and were doing nonlegal work. Most had either started their own businesses or gone into family businesses. Few had been hired by anyone other than their relatives. If you are considering making a complete switch to a nonlegal career, you might want to conduct your own study to gauge your chances in your own community. Be advised that one difficulty in conducting such a study is defining "nonlegal" work. For example, is a lawyer who becomes a claims adjuster doing "nonlegal" work? Another difficulty is government work. Some lawyers are able to land nonlegal government jobs, but you cannot tell whether they did so on their own merits or through political connections.

In August 1990 I was hired as a paralegal at the Aetna Life and Casualty Company's home office in Hartford. I sought this job because it would enable me to get my foot in the door of a large, nonlegal employer. Aetna had 12,000 employees in Hartford, most of whom did nonlegal work. I was hoping to make contacts which would enable me to maneuver into a nonlegal position at Aetna and never again have to work as a lawyer or legal assistant.

Then a miracle happened. It was August 9, 1990, my first day at Aetna. It was 4:30 p.m., and I was about to go home. I had spent the day doing legal research, writing a memo, and discussing the memo with my boss. I had enjoyed the day very much. My boss told me that every day would be like this. Suddenly, I was overcome with a strange feeling I had never experienced in all my years as a lawyer and had thought would be impossible for me to experience: contentment with a legal job.

As the weeks and months passed, I was having a ball with this $13-an-hour paralegal job in which no one bothered me, no one lied to me, no one tried to use me to gain an unfair advantage over another, no one demanded that I be in two or three places at once, and no one stiffed me for money. I had no moral dilemmas, ethical dilemmas, or malpractice worries. The work was relaxing. I did not feel drained at the end of the day. I had time and energy to go out at night and on weekends, get involved in civic activities, and enjoy life. I did not feel a desperate need for a vacation. In short, it was nothing like retail law practice. I felt rejuvenated. It was as though my entire legal career had been born again.

A peaceful, easy feeling

My boss, a nonlawyer, was amazed at my zeal for legal research and writing. He asked me why I enjoyed doing that more than practicing law. His question harkened me back to a late, lonely Saturday night back in 1976 in the Washington University law library. I was in the stacks, cite-checking an article for the law review, when the editor-in-chief walked by, told me he appreciated my working so late on a Saturday to help meet a deadline, and said, "Dave, I don't understand you. You don't seem to give a damn about your courses, but you're one of the hardest-working law review staffers. Can you explain that?"

My explanation went something like this: "Here in the law library, no one is hassling me. No professor is trying to intimidate me, no classmate is showing off how much he knows, and no one is giving me a three-hour exam to see if I understand this article. The law library is an oasis, a temple of calm and reason and reflection." Then, borrowing from an Eagles song that was popular back then, I told him that the law library gave me a "peaceful, easy feeling."

So that's what I told my boss at Aetna: "Doing legal research and then sitting at the computer and writing a memo about it gives me a peaceful, easy feeling."

Researching some workers' compensation issues at Aetna led to my interest in the related field of employment law. By late 1991, I had become fascinated with such topics as disability discrimination (the new Americans with Disabilities Act was a hot topic), sexual harassment (the Clarence Thomas confirmation hearings were in October 1991), and the Civil Rights Act of 1991 (which took effect in November 1991). Unfortunately, there were no employment law opportunities for me at Aetna—only workers' compensation and other insurance-related matters. The Aetna law department was downsizing.

So I began to think the unthinkable: returning to private law practice. But when I say private, I don't mean retail. Retail was still unthinkable as far as I was concerned. In December 1991, I left Aetna and opened a modest (150 square feet in a suite with three other lawyers) law office in Springfield, and began the wholesale law practice that now inspires this book.

Starting with confidence

The rest of the book will tell you why retail lawyers need wholesale lawyers; how wholesale lawyers fill that need; what the ethical considerations are; and how you can start, manage, market, and prosper in your own wholesale law practice. But first I want to address three quandaries mentioned earlier that I have not yet addressed in this overview. I will address them only briefly, for their outcome will vary with the individual, and my own experience might not be particularly relevant.

First is the image quandary: What will your fellow lawyers, retail clients, family, and friends think of your decision to switch from retail to wholesale law practice? I call this the "Fighter-to-Writer Syndrome." A lawyer is supposed to be a fighter, someone who fights for justice. I was a fighter when I was a retail lawyer, and I worried that becoming a writer (which is what wholesale lawyers mostly do) would diminish my fighter image. I no longer care about that image. When I tell people (lawyers and nonlawyers alike) that I do research, writing, and consulting for other lawyers rather than representing clients and fighting courtroom battles, their reaction is nearly always positive, and sometimes even admiring. They see me as a lawyer's lawyer. That's the image I prefer.

The image quandary is somewhat related to the obscurity quandary (Will you labor in obscurity?). Ironically, I am more visible in wholesale law practice than I was in retail law practice. As a wholesaler, I have argued cases in the U.S. Court of Appeals[11] and the Massachusetts Supreme Judicial Court;[12] assisted many of the best small-firm trial lawyers in exciting, high-stakes cases in which opposing counsel were from the biggest and best law firms in Boston and Springfield; spoken on employment law at many seminars; and published numerous articles.[13] I did not have as many such opportunities in retail law practice. I call this the "Dennis Eckersley Effect," named for a baseball pitcher who achieved greater glory in his supporting role as a relief pitcher than he did in his leading role as a starting pitcher. It has happened to me because, quite frankly, I think my fellow lawyers appreciate me more than my retail clients did. If you like to feel appreciated, you will like wholesale law practice.

Finally, the income quandary: Will you earn as much money in wholesale law practice as you would in retail practice? My income (revenue minus office expenses) is still about what it would be if I were a high school teacher with the same length of service (nineteen years) as I have in law. But don't draw any conclusions from my income. Some of you will make much more than I do, some will make less. You might be able to earn more per hour or per case than I do and be less fussy about the types of cases you accept than I am, in which case you will earn more money than I do. As I explain in Chapter 5, with a good mix of hourly work and contingent-fee cases, a wholesale lawyer can earn a decent living.

The road is at an end, and you have reached your destination: the wonderful world of wholesale law practice. Your guidebook to that world lies ahead.

Notes

1. 1 *Law Office Econ. & Mgmt. Man.* §11:06 (Deerfield, IL: Clark Boardman Callaghan 1995 supp.), *citing* William I. Weston, "Temporary Lawyers to the . . . Rescue?" 5 *Compleat Lawyer* 38 (Fall 1988). However, the ethical opinion

which governs "temporary lawyers"—*ABA Comm. on Ethics and Professional Responsibility,* Formal Op. 356 (1988) (reprinted in Appendix A)—also governs contract and wholesale lawyers.

2. Robb Mandelbaum, "Temporary Relief," *CCM—The American Lawyer's Corporate Counsel Magazine,* Sept. 1995, at 105; *see also N.Y. L.J.,* Nov. 13, 1995, at 3 (ad for Special Counsel International, an employment agency which places temporary lawyers with law firms and corporate legal departments, lists hourly fees of $45 to $125); *id.,* Nov. 6, 1995, at 5 (ad for Co-Counsel, another such agency, lists hourly fees of $35 to $125 an hour); Richard J. Block, "Temporary Help Provides Both Talent and Savings," *Nat'l L.J.,* Oct. 17, 1994, at C27 ("in-house counsel can enlist the services of a temporary attorney through a placement agency and pay between $125 to $150 per hour.")

3. *Legal Recruiters 1996 Directory,* supp. to *Am. Lawyer,* Jan./Feb. 1996.

4. Robb Mandelbaum, "Temporary Relief," *CCM—The American Lawyer's Corporate Counsel Magazine,* Sept. 1995, at 105.

5. *Legal Recruiters 1996 Directory,* supp. to *Am. Lawyer,* Jan./Feb. 1996, inside back cover.

6. Samuel A. Frederick, "Teaming Up With Temporary Lawyers," in "Litigation at a Crossroads," supp. to *Am. Lawyer,* May 1995, at 61 (*quoting* Robert Abrahams of 155-lawyer Schulte, Roth & Zabel).

7. Deborah Arron, "Well-Chosen Contract Work is a Springboard," *Nat'l L.J.,* Aug. 14, 1995, at C4 ("corporate legal departments . . . provide the lion's share of revenue to the nation's temporary placement agencies."); Samuel A. Frederick, "Controlling Compensation Costs by Using Temporary Attorneys," *Law Prac. Mgmt.,* July/Aug. 1995, at 34.

8. 1980 *Am. B. Found. Res. J.* 926, 928.

9. John P. Heinz & Edward O. Laumann, *Chicago Lawyers: The Social Structure of the Bar* 195 (New York & Chicago: Russell Sage Found. and Am. B. Found. 1982).

10. Andrea Sachs, "Have Law Degree, Will Travel," *Time,* Dec. 11, 1989, at 106.

11. *Armstrong v. Jefferson Smurfit Corp.,* 30 F.3d 11 (1st Cir. 1994).

12. *Draghetti v. Chmielewski,* 626 N.E. 2d 862 (Mass. 1994).

13. *E.g.,* "Discovery of the Plaintiff's Mental Health History in an Employment Discrimination Case," 16 *W. New Eng. L. Rev.* 55 (1994).

CHAPTER 1

Why Retail Lawyers Need Wholesale Lawyers

The vast majority of lawyers in private practice are retail lawyers: they make their living advising and representing clients directly. The exceptions are wholesale lawyers, temporary lawyers, and those law firm associates who have little or no client contact.

Half the lawyers in private practice are sole practitioners.[1] Another 10 percent are in firms of two to five lawyers.[2] With approximately 600,000 lawyers in active, private practice today,[3] that means there are approximately 360,000 lawyers who practice solo or in firms of five or fewer lawyers. These 360,000 will be collectively referred to as "small-firm lawyers."

The needs of small-firm lawyers

Small-firm retail lawyers have a great need for wholesale lawyers because small-firm lawyers generally have to do their own legal research and writing. They have no one else to do it for them; and most cannot afford to hire a full-time or even part-time associate to do it for them.

It is a time-consuming task. Next to client contact and miscellaneous telephone contact, legal research and writing consume more of the average lawyer's time than any other activity, according to a 1990 ABA survey.[4]

Therein lies the opportunity for freelance, specialized legal researchers/writers/consultants. In any given lawsuit or other type of legal dispute or transaction, a wholesale lawyer can be to a retail lawyer what a top-notch, specialized associate often is to a partner in a large law firm: a $35-an-hour writer and advisor[5] ($35 an hour, eight hours a day, five days a week, fifty weeks a year, amounts to $70,000, which is what a starting associate at a very large law firm typically earns). But where the partner must pay the associate a full-time salary plus benefits every week, the small-firm retail lawyer need only pay the wholesale lawyer for the time the wholesale lawyer spends on that one legal matter (say, $35 an hour), or pay the wholesale lawyer a contingent fee (say, one-third of whatever fee the retail lawyer earns on the matter), or pay a mixed hourly/contingent fee (say, $20 an hour plus 20 percent of the fee). Wholesale lawyers have very low overhead and therefore are willing and able to work for lower hourly fees, especially if they occasionally earn some big money in contingent-fee cases.

Like the large-firm associate, the wholesale lawyer is more than just a workhorse. She is an alter ego, a second brain, another set of eyes and ears to the retail lawyer she is assisting. Even the most brilliant retail lawyer cannot think of everything. The wholesale lawyer will think of factual and legal issues the retail lawyer has missed, correct the retail lawyer's mistakes, and provide the retail lawyer with objectivity. The wholesale lawyer is to the retail lawyer what the trainer is to the boxer, the editor is to the author, the campaign manager is to the political candidate. The synergism between two people working toward a common goal is empowering, enlightening, and enjoyable to both. Simply put, two heads are better than one.

Unfortunately, few of the 360,000 small-firm lawyers have a second "head" to work with. They might have a lawyer-friend down the hall they can "bounce ideas off" from time to time, but they have no one who is fully knowledgeable about the particular case or transaction they are handling and truly motivated to help them with it. Even small-firm lawyers who have partners often have no one to brainstorm with about a particular case or transaction. Many small-firm partnerships are really just office-sharing arrangements in which the partners share space, expenses, malpractice liability, and the firm name, but not revenues. Each partner has his or her own clients, is paid only what he or she brings in, and has little or no incentive to get involved in another partner's case or transaction.

The only type of lawyer who has the incentive to get *fully* involved in another lawyer's case or transaction is one with a *financial* incentive to do so, one who earns money helping other lawyers. Only law firm associates, revenue-sharing partners, and wholesale lawyers have such an incentive.

A small-firm lawyer, by using the services of a specialized wholesale lawyer, can achieve the same efficiency and quality work product as a large law firm does, at least in those cases where the small-firm lawyer has a good basic understanding of the subject matter of the case but does not have the resources (partners, associates, and support staff) the large firm has.

Oral advocacy and written advocacy: two different skills

Two underlying problems give rise to the need for wholesale lawyers. One is that retail law practice is more conducive to *speaking* than it is to research and writing. Retail lawyers spend most of the day speaking—on the phone, in meetings with clients or adversaries, or in court—and they speak at frequent intervals during the day. They rarely have a long stretch of quiet, uninterrupted time to concentrate on complex research and writing tasks. Legal research and writing require longer periods of concentration than speaking does. Having to alternate back and forth from speaking to research and writing each day—which is what most retail lawyers do—makes it virtually impossible for retail lawyers to do their best research and writing.

The other problem is that many retail lawyers cannot write well or do effective legal research even when they have sufficient time. They may be outstanding orators, but speaking is a rather different skill than research and writing are. That is why some great courtroom lawyers are poor brief writers and some great brief writers are poor courtroom lawyers.

Whether due to their lack of quiet time or lack of skill, retail lawyers, particularly small-firm retail lawyers who have no associates, often cut corners on their research and writing, hoping, like retailers of goods often do, that their oral skills and compelling personalities will carry their arguments.

Written advocacy: the principal tool of the lawyer's trade

Unfortunately for these retail lawyers, *written* advocacy is what wins most legal disputes and facilitates most legal transactions. The written word is the principal tool of the lawyer's trade.[6] Except in some criminal and domestic cases, and the tiny percentage of civil cases that actually go to trial, written advocacy—demand letters, pleadings, interrogatories, carefully-crafted deposition questions, jury instructions, briefs, opinion letters, settlement proposals, contracts, and the like—is the engine that drives the wheels of justice. Nearly all legal disputes and legal transactions are handled primarily on paper and finalized on paper. William Prosser remarked that "the average lawyer writes more than the average novelist."[7] Texas Supreme Court Chief Justice Thomas R. Phillips says, "[M]ost lawyers, Perry Mason and Court TV notwithstanding, do their most important communication through the written word. The heart of most lawyers' work comes not in a rousing jury summation, but in the daily preparation of a ground lease, or an SEC S-3, or a routine request for production of documents."[8]

In litigation, good writing is more important than ever before. Because of clogged court dockets, state and federal judges are increasingly deciding motions "on the papers" without oral argument. "If you haven't sold them on the papers, you are history most of the time," says Peter Davis, a partner at Oakland, California's Crosby, Heafey, Roach & May, which has a former magazine editor on staff as an in-house writing guru.[9] "Good, clear writing wins cases," says former University of Virginia law professor C. Edward Good, now "writer-in-residence" at Washington, D.C.'s Finnegan, Henderson, Farabow, Garratt & Dunner.[10]

The law of comparative advantage

Retail lawyers need wholesale lawyers because wholesale lawyers have what an economist would call a *comparative advantage* when it comes to legal research and writing. The law of comparative advantage holds that an entity should produce what it is best suited to produce, and should purchase from others what it is least suited to produce. In 1990s business terminology, this is called outsourcing.[11] Retail lawyers can often serve their clients better by outsourcing research and writing tasks to wholesale lawyers.

The need for specialized wholesale lawyers

Wholesale lawyers who specialize in one or a few substantive areas of law are particularly helpful to retail lawyers. In 1979, when I entered solo practice after working for a sole practitioner my first two years out of law school, I placed an ad in *Massachusetts Lawyers Weekly* offering "research and briefs" for $12 an hour. No one called me. One reason, a lawyer explained to me, was that lawyers reading the ad probably realized I was a recent law school grad who knew little about any particular area of law and would have to reinvent the wheel every time I was assigned a project.

But a *specialized* wholesale lawyer, one with mastery in, say, bankruptcy, real estate, personal injury, intellectual property, labor and employment, health care, environmental law, divorce, probate, estate planning, taxation, collections, contracts, or corporate law, can be in great demand. Chapter 4 explains in greater detail why wholesale lawyers should specialize and how they can learn a specialty if they do not already have one.

The need for flexible fee arrangements

Another reason my 1979 ad was a flop was that lawyers were reluctant to pay $12 an hour (which, with inflation, is like $35 an hour in 1996) out of their pockets when representing plaintiffs in contingent-fee cases. They did not want to risk losing more money than they had to if the case lost. They wanted a wholesale lawyer who was willing to share the risk with them, just as their clients wanted a retail lawyer who was willing to share the risk, which is basically what a contingent fee is. Chapter 5 discusses flexible fee arrangements between wholesale and retail lawyers.

Of course, a small-firm lawyer always has the option of referring the client to a specialized retail lawyer, who will represent the client and, where permitted by ethical codes, pay the small-firm lawyer a referral fee. That can be an excellent arrangement, if that's what the small-firm lawyer really wants to do. However, with clients scarce these days (because they are spread among so many retail lawyers), many small-firm lawyers do not want to refer clients. They want to keep clients for themselves. Wholesale lawyers, who have little or no desire to represent clients directly, enable small firms to keep the clients and keep the lion's share of the fee.

The need for personalized service

There are also national legal research and writing firms that a small-firm lawyer can call. However, most retail lawyers want *personalized* service. They want to be able to meet with and speak frequently with their researcher/writer and want their researcher/writer to speak with the client in order, for example, to obtain answers to interrogatories, gather the necessary facts to draft a complaint or a contract, prepare for a deposition, or review documents. Legal research is driven by the specific facts in each case, which are best known to the lawyers closely involved in that case,[12] namely, the retail lawyer and the freelance associate—the wholesale lawyer. In short, retail lawyers want their researcher/writer to be as accessible and useful to them in that particular case as a partner, associate, or legal assistant would be.

The needs of large law firms and in-house corporate legal departments

Although small-firm retail lawyers have, in general, a greater need for wholesale lawyers than large-firm lawyers do, large-firm lawyers may have an occasional need for wholesale lawyers. If, for example, a client who the firm wishes to please is unable to pay the firm $10,000 (50 hours at $200 an hour) for a research/writing project, and the firm does not wish to pull an associate off better-paying matters to do this project, the firm might wish to enlist a wholesale lawyer to ghostwrite the project for $1,750 (50 hours at $35 an hour). Wholesale lawyers can perform the same function for large law firms and in-house corporate legal departments that lawyers from temp agencies now perform.

The needs of small in-house corporate and municipal legal departments

Lawyers in small in-house corporate legal departments and small municipal legal departments often have the same problem small-firm private practitioners have: they must do their own legal research and writing. Moreover, they often lack the expertise to handle a matter completely in house. If, however, they feel reasonably comfortable handling a matter in house but need *some* outside expertise, it might be more cost effective for them to hire a wholesale lawyer than an outside law firm.

The future need for wholesale lawyers

The need for wholesale lawyers will grow rapidly over the next few years because the small-firm lawyer population is the fastest-growing segment of the legal profession. Large law firms as a whole have only slightly grown in the past few years. The total number of lawyers in the 250 largest U.S. law firms increased only 5.1% (from 68,397 to 71,918) from 1991 to 1996, and some of that increase is due to law firms including contract lawyers when reporting their total number of lawyers.[13] There has been little, if any, growth in the number of government and in-house corporate lawyers. The poor job market for recent law-school graduates and experienced lawyers laid off by law firms and corporate legal departments has caused many such lawyers to open their own small practices.[14] Because law schools continue to produce some 40,000 new lawyers each year (although some law schools have recently reduced the size of their entering classes),[15] and because private, small-firm practice is the only way a lawyer without a job can practice law, small-firm practice is where most of the growth is today in the legal profession. The larger the small-firm lawyer population, the larger the need for wholesale lawyers.

Notes

1. Marianne Lavelle, "Lawyers Are Top Earners," *Nat'l L.J.*, Aug. 28, 1995, at A22, cl. 2 (estimating that 54 percent of private lawyers were solo in 1995); *Lawyer Statistical Report* 7 (estimating that 45 percent of private lawyers were solo in 1991).

2. *Lawyer Statistical Report* 7; "A Paper for the Unsung Small Firms," *N.Y. Times,* Mar. 12, 1993, B14, cl. 4 (estimating that two-thirds of all lawyers work in firms of five or fewer lawyers); Cameron C. Gamble, "What Can the Organized Bar Do to Serve the Solo and Small Firm General Practitioner?" 68 *Fla. B.J.* 20 (Jan. 1994) ("Almost 80 percent of lawyers in private practice are solos or in small firms.").

3. *Lawyer Statistical Report* 7; *Occupational Outlook Handbook* 115 (Washington: U.S. Dept. of Labor 1994–95 ed.).

4. *The State of the Legal Profession 1990* 15 (Chicago: ABA 1991).

5. *See* Kevin A. Kordana, "Law Firms and Associate Careers: Tournament Theory Versus the Production-Imperative Model," 104 *Yale L.J.* 1907, 1925 (1995):

> While the "paperwork" must be done correctly and with attention to detail, the demands in terms of skills and (especially) experience are not such that clients are willing to pay for this work to be done by partners charging a high hourly rate. . . . Therefore, in order to maximize profits, the partner will personally handle the strategic work and will employ one or more associates to do the paperwork.

(quotes in original).

6. Honorable Domenick L. Gabrielli, "The Importance of Research and Legal Writing in the Law School Education," 46 *Alb. L. Rev.* 1, 4 (1981) ("Wielding the written word is a lawyer's prime tool.").

7. *Quoted in* Frederick G. Gale & Joseph M. Moxley, *How to Write the Winning Brief* 1 (Chicago: ABA, 1992); *see also* Bryan A. Garner, *The Elements of Legal Style* 3 (New York: Oxford, 1991) ("law is a literary profession").

8. *Quoted in* Terri LeClercq, *Expert Legal Writing* ix (Austin, Tex.: Univ. Of Texas Press 1995).

9. Richard B. Schmitt, "Law Schools, Firms Sending a Message: Polish Your Prose," *Wall Street Journal,* Aug. 28, 1995, at B3, cl. 1.

10. *Ibid.*

11. "Outsourcing" has been defined as "the payment to outside businesses for specialized services as they become necessary." Bruce Berman, "Firms Need to Back Up Consultants," *Nat'l L.J.,* Jan. 9, 1995, at B9.

12. *See* Amy Stevens, "Law Firm Fat Threatened By Lean Network," *Wall Street Journal,* July 8, 1994, at B8 (remarks of Doug Kranwinkle, managing partner of O'Melveny & Myers's New York office, on limitations of using national research companies); *see also* D.M. Osborne, "Should You Be Afraid of This Man?" *Am. Lawyer,* June 1995, at 70. "This man" is Dov Seidman, head of Legal Research Network, Inc. The article states:

> [E]ven some of Seidman's supporters point out limitations in LRN's approach. While LRN customers get the benefit of an expert researcher, they forfeit direct interaction between the researcher and the lawyer responsible for rendering advice, for example. "You don't get the opportunity to plumb the mind of the researcher," notes Mobil assistant general counsel Douglas McDougall, whose concern was echoed by several of the firm lawyers interviewed.

13. Chris Klein, "More Lawyers Than Ever in 250 Largest Law Firms," *Nat'l L.J.,* Sept. 30, 1996, at C2, cl. 1.

14. Barbara L. Morganstern, "Solo Network: Top Bananas Turn Rainmakers," 82 *A.B.A. J.* 92 (Mar. 1996); Scott Medintz, "A Shingle of One's Own," *Am. Lawyer,* Mar. 1995, at 56; Amy Stevens, "Lawyer With Six Years of Experience, Top Credentials, Seeks Job, Any Job at All," Wall Street Journal, July 22,

1994, at B1; Susan Ferraro, "Risks and Rewards in Leaving Big Firms for Small Practices," *N.Y. Times*, July 22, 1994, at B9.

15. However, a number of law schools are voluntarily reducing the size of their entering class as a moral or ethical response to the glutted market for lawyers. Patricia G. Barnes, "Cutting Classes: Many Law Schools Are Shrinking Along With the Job Market," 81 *A.B.A.J.* 26 (Dec. 1995).

CHAPTER 2

What Does a Wholesale Lawyer Do?

A freelance associate

What does a wholesale lawyer do? A wholesale lawyer does whatever the retail lawyer asks him or her to do and the wholesale lawyer is willing to do. Their relationship is limited only by their imagination and personal preferences, and by the legal and ethical constraints imposed on all lawyers. The wholesale lawyer is like a freelance associate. The wholesale lawyer does whatever the retail lawyer would ask an associate to do if the retail lawyer had an associate; if the retail lawyer does have an associate, the wholesale lawyer is like an additional associate.

There are, of course, some obvious technical distinctions between an associate and a wholesale lawyer. The wholesale lawyer is not an employee of the retail lawyer, but is rather an independent contractor who usually does not work a regular schedule for the retail lawyer and usually works for other retail lawyers at the same time. The retail lawyer pays the wholesale lawyer either an hourly fee, a fixed fee, a contingent fee, or some combination; not wages or salary. The fees that retail lawyers pay wholesale lawyers are discussed in Chapter 5. The wholesale lawyer usually has less contact with clients and adversaries than an associate does.

The initial consultation with the retail lawyer

Here's an example of how my wholesale practice works. A lawyer will call me and say, "Dave, I've got a client coming in who says she's being sexually harassed at work. Can you come by to hear her story?" I go to the lawyer's office and meet with the lawyer and the client. The lawyer usually introduces me to the client as an "employment law specialist" or "consultant to other lawyers." After we talk to the client, the lawyer and I talk to each other to size up the case, and if the lawyer decides to take the case (the retail lawyer makes that decision, not I, although I do offer my opinion), the lawyer and I discuss how I will be paid. If I really like the case, and if the lawyer wants to charge the client a contingent fee, I will usually agree to a contingent fee for myself: one-third (or sometimes one-fourth, or as much as one-half, depending on how much the lawyer will be depending on my services) of the lawyer's fee. If we are defending a case, I charge the lawyer a straight hourly fee ($35 per hour).

Preparation of documents

I write (including drafting, typing, and preparing in final form ready for signature) all the documents in the case, subject to whatever changes the retail lawyer wishes. For example, when assisting a plaintiff's lawyer, I write the complaint, the plaintiff's interrogatories to the defendant, the plaintiff's answers to the defendant's interrogatories (I usually meet with the client for a few hours in the lawyer's office to obtain these answers), deposition questions, motions, settlement proposals, summary judgment materials, pretrial memoranda, jury instructions, and any other necessary documents.

A ghostwriter, for the most part

Except in rare circumstances, I do not put my name on these documents. I put the retail lawyer's name on them and he or she signs them. I rarely file an appearance in a case, take or defend a deposition, negotiate with opposing counsel, or try cases in court. These are retail functions, and I prefer the retail lawyer to perform them.

I do, however, attend many depositions and trials, during which I advise and assist the retail lawyer. I am mainly the retail lawyer's ghostwriter[1] and advisor. I don't want the responsibility of being attorney of record in dozens of cases for dozens of different lawyers, some of whom are more capable than others. That would make me as responsible for the client as the retail lawyer is, which I do not wish to be. It would increase my malpractice exposure. If the client were to fire the retail lawyer, or if the retail lawyer were to withdraw, I would be stuck with the client and the case. Also, sometimes I write nasty (but never unethical) things in briefs, pleadings, and letters to which I personally would not want to sign my name, but that the retail lawyer nevertheless wants me to write. If the retail lawyer wants to sign these documents, that is his or her business.

Basically, I want the court, the client, and the opposition to know that the client is being represented by the retail lawyer, not by me. Once in a while, if the retail lawyer insists, I will argue a summary judgment motion or other dispositive motion, or an appeal, in court because I am usually more conversant in the technicalities of employment law than the retail lawyer is (which is why the retail lawyer hired me in the first place).

But this is merely my personal preference. A retail lawyer and a wholesale lawyer might prefer the wholesale lawyer to take a more visible, adversarial role than I wish to take. For example, some wholesale lawyers want their names (along with the retail lawyer's name) on briefs they write. They don't want to *ghost*write. Personally, I have no problem with the retail lawyer taking all the credit and relegating me to ghostdom. After all, it is the retail lawyer who attracts the client in the first place, deals with the client on a regular basis through thick and thin, and is ultimately responsible for the client.

Then again, some retail lawyers want to give the wholesale lawyer credit. They want the wholesale lawyer's name to appear on pleadings. They want the wholesale lawyer to attend settlement conferences. They want to brag to the opposing party that a specialist is helping them. The wholesale lawyer can be a status symbol!

"Soup-to-nuts" or "à la carte" service

Some retail lawyers don't need (or don't want to pay for) full soup-to-nuts service in a case, but instead want à la carte service. They want the wholesale lawyer merely to critique a complaint they wrote or write a brief in opposition to a summary judgment motion or advise them whether to accept a particular settlement offer. For these services, the wholesale lawyer charges an hourly fee, a fixed fee, or, by mutual agreement, a low percentage of the retail lawyer's fee. Occasionally retail lawyers will ask wholesale lawyers if they have already written a brief on a particular topic. If they have, they can sell the brief for, say, $100 or $200, depending on the length and complexity of the brief.

Some retail lawyers try to refer clients whom they do not wish to represent at all to the wholesale lawyer. They want the wholesale lawyer to represent the client all by himself. This is up to the wholesale lawyer. If he wants to represent the client, fine; if he does not want to, he is free to tell the retail lawyer that he (the wholesale lawyer) is in the business of helping lawyers represent their own clients, not representing clients himself, and politely decline.

Wholesale lawyers spend a good deal of time on the phone answering questions from other lawyers but nowhere near as much time as retail lawyers spend on the phone with clients, and wholesale lawyers can usually confine their teleconferences to a certain time of day. Whether they charge for these calls is up to them. I usually do not charge for these calls unless I have spent at least an hour, cumulatively, with a particular lawyer on a particular matter. I want to encourage lawyers to call me. Many of them will someday send me a research/writing assignment or refer another lawyer to me, and I'll make some money.

Long, gentle, flexible hours

I work very long hours, but they are flexible, low-pressure, no-aggravation hours. I spend about fifteen hours a week in the offices of the retail lawyers I serve, talking to them and their clients, screening new cases, and reading files. I spend another ten hours a week in the law library. I was spending thirty hours a week in the law library when I started my wholesale law practice, but over time I have developed a large inventory of forms and briefs on virtually every employment law topic, which cuts down my library time. I'm sure you can achieve the same efficiency. I diligently keep up with all new employment law developments. I spend about thirty hours a week at my word processor, writing for retail lawyers. I do much of this writing at home, evenings and weekends. That is a major advantage of wholesale law practice: the hours are flexible and most of the work can be done wherever your laptop will fit.

Life as a wholesale lawyer is similar to life as a law professor or appellate judge. For ten to fifteen hours a week, they must be in a certain place: the wholesale lawyer in other lawyers' offices, the law professor in class, and the judge in court. Then they spend long, gentle, flexible hours engaged in legal research, legal writing, and collegial legal discussions.

The customer (the retail lawyer) is always right

By virtue of the fact that the retail lawyer is always in charge and can overrule the wholesale lawyer, I, as a wholesale lawyer, live by the adage, "The retail lawyer is always right." A retail lawyer (or any professional, for that matter) cannot live by that adage when dealing with clients or patients. Doctors, lawyers, and CPAs must exercise independent professional judgment. If a medical patient wants to undergo an operation that his or her doctor thinks is contrary to the patient's medical interests, the doctor should not perform the operation. Similarly, a lawyer must exercise independent professional judgment and say no to clients who make irrational or unethical demands. Unfortunately, saying no to a client creates tension in the lawyer-client relationship. When I was a retail lawyer, many of my intense, gut-wrenching arguments were not with adversaries or in open court, but rather with my own clients.

I don't have this problem in wholesale law practice. The retail lawyer is always the boss. I advise retail lawyers how I think matters should be handled, and I try gently to persuade them to see and do things differently when I think they are wrong. But they are mature professionals, and if they disagree with me, that is their prerogative. They hire me to help them accomplish their objectives, not mine. So long as they are not acting illegally or unethically, nor asking me to act illegally or unethically, I do what they ask me to do.

If you like being the ultimate decisionmaker—the one in charge—don't become a wholesale lawyer. But if you like to have "influence without authority" (the title of a best-selling management book a few years ago), then do become a wholesale lawyer. Ironically, even though I am never in charge, I usually get my way: the retail lawyers follow my advice far more often than they reject it.

Litigating against the Flat-Earth Society: when bureaucrats and opposing counsel protest the wholesaler's role

Once in a while I encounter bureaucrats or opposing lawyers who either don't understand my role in a case or simply object to it. For example, a retail lawyer (let's call him Plaintiff's Counsel) asked me to help him with an age-discrimination case. Defense Counsel had scheduled a deposition of the plaintiff for the next day, at Defense Counsel's office. Plaintiff's Counsel wanted me to attend, observe, and provide Plaintiff's Counsel with advice, although Plaintiff's Counsel would actually handle the deposition. Defense Counsel did not know I was advising Plaintiff's Counsel. I had not filed an appearance in the case, and I did not plan to. There is no ethical requirement that a retail lawyer disclose to opposing counsel that the retail lawyer has retained the services of a wholesale lawyer.

Plaintiff's Counsel, the plaintiff, and I show up for the deposition. Defense Counsel, who knows me, asks, "David, what are you doing here?" Here's what followed:

David:	"I'm here to assist Plaintiff's Counsel."
Defense Counsel:	"Have you filed an appearance?"
David:	"No."
Defense Counsel:	"Then you can't attend the deposition."
David:	"But I won't be saying anything. Plaintiff's Counsel will do all the talking, except that I'll talk to him once in a while. Rule 30 [Fed.R.Civ.P. 30] does not give you the right to bar me from the deposition."
Defense Counsel:	"Nor does it give you the right to attend. I'm afraid I must insist that you leave. It's nothing personal, David."

(In anticipation that this might happen sometime, I had photocop-

ied a page from a deposition manual—I could find no cases on point—that states that a lawyer can bring a "legal assistant" to a deposition, and kept it in my briefcase. I showed this page to Defense Counsel.)

David:	"I'm Plaintiff's Counsel's 'legal assistant' today."
Defense Counsel:	"You're not a legal assistant, you're a lawyer."
David:	"All lawyers are 'legal assistants.' "
Defense Counsel:	"And I suppose you type for Plaintiff's Counsel as well."
David:	"I do in this case."

Defense Counsel let me stay.

Then there was the unemployment compensation hearing that reminded me of second grade, when the teacher intercepted a note I had passed to another kid. The employee's lawyer asked me to attend the hearing to see if I thought the employee had a viable wrongful termination claim, and to provide advice. Here's what happened:

Hearing Officer:	"Who's representing the employee?"
Employee's Lawyer:	"I am."
Hearing Officer [looking at me]:	"Who are you?"
David:	"I'm Attorney David Robinson. I am assisting Employee's Lawyer."
Hearing Officer:	"Why? Does he need help?"
David:	"I don't know if he needs help, but I am an employment law consultant to other lawyers, and Employee's Lawyer might want to consult with me during the hearing."
Hearing Officer:	"I don't think you need to be here, Mr. Robinson. If you want, you can sit in the back of the room, as an observer."

(Rather than argue with Hearing Officer, I did sit in the back of the room and kept my mouth shut, but at one point I handed a

note to Employee's Lawyer suggesting a question that I thought he should ask Employer.)

Defense Counsel: "Objection! The observer just handed a note to Employee's Lawyer!"

Hearing Officer: "That was inappropriate, Mr. Robinson. Let me see that note."

Employee's Lawyer: "Excuse me, but that note is a privileged communication to me. With all due respect, I don't think I should have to show it to you."

David: "I don't mind if Hearing Officer sees the note."

(Employee's Lawyer handed Hearing Officer the note, which contained a perfectly legitimate question. Hearing Officer nevertheless scolded me for passing the note.)

David: "I've seen employers bring three lawyers from a big law firm to represent them at these hearings. Why can't a sole practitioner like Employee's Lawyer bring another lawyer to consult with?"

Hearing Officer: "Because they're all in the same firm. Are you in Employee's Lawyer's firm?"

David: "He doesn't have a firm. That's the whole point. He's trying to gain the same advantage a firm has."

Hearing Officer: "I still think you shouldn't pass notes. It's undignified."

But such episodes are rare. The vast majority of judges and opposing lawyers, including lawyers from very large firms, understand and respect the wholesale lawyer's role. They respect the small-firm lawyer's efforts to level the playing field against large firms that have specialists. As wholesale law practice becomes more widespread, there will be even fewer episodes such as these.

Note

1. On the topic of legal ghostwriting, *see generally* Darlene Ricker, "Verbatim" ("Taking the Words Right Out of Their Mouths: Some Tips on How to Be a Friendly Ghost"), 22 *Student Lawyer* 9 (Feb. 1994).

CHAPTER 3

Ethical Considerations in Wholesale Law Practice

The wholesale lawyer's identity

Wholesale lawyers, just like lawyers who sell their services directly to the public, are bound by the ethical code governing practitioners in the jurisdiction where they are licensed. Neither the ABA Model Rules of Professional Conduct nor the predecessor Code of Professional Responsibility make a distinction between lawyers who work in private practice settings and those who do not provide retail services to clients. Licensed wholesale lawyers must abide by the rules or face disciplinary sanction.

Although the ethical rules do not exempt wholesale lawyers from their strictures, the rules were clearly not drafted with wholesale lawyers in mind. Many of the rules deal specifically with the lawyer's duties to actual clients, rather than indirectly to clients through other lawyers. Also, the fact that the number of wholesale lawyers is relatively small means that there are not many complaints against wholesale lawyers. As a result, no identifiable body of case law or commentary discusses how the rules should be applied to wholesale lawyers.

This chapter addresses some of the more common ethical issues for wholesale lawyers, and offers some suggestions on how to act in situations where ethical rules come into play. There are, of course, other ethical issues that could arise and are not addressed here. Wholesale lawyers need to have a working knowledge of the ethical rules in their states and a sensitivity to ethical questions as they arise in the context of actual cases. Such advance preparation is probably the best defense against unintentional, but possibly catastrophic ethical errors.

Sometimes a retail lawyer does not want a client to know that a wholesale lawyer is working on the case. The retail lawyer wants to impress the client, which means conveying the impression that the retail lawyer is the genius behind the great pleadings and letters being generated on the client's behalf. Does the retail lawyer have an ethical obligation to disclose to the client that a wholesale lawyer is involved?

The answer depends on (1) how closely the retail lawyer is supervising the wholesale lawyer's work and (2) whether the retail lawyer is splitting the fee with the wholesale lawyer. If the retail lawyer is closely supervising the wholesale lawyer's work and is paying the wholesaler a flat or hourly fee (as opposed to charging it to the client or paying the wholesaler a percentage of the fee received from the client), there is no duty to disclose to the client that a wholesale lawyer is working on the case. The ABA had occasion to consider this issue in 1988, and issued Formal Opinion 356. Although Formal Op. 356 uses the term "temporary lawyer," a temporary lawyer does the same type of work a wholesale lawyer does, so the opinion governs wholesale lawyers as well. The rationale is that a wholesale lawyer is so closely associated with the retail lawyer in that particular client's case that the retail lawyer should have no greater duty to disclose that a wholesale lawyer has written the pleadings than if an associate, secretary, or paralegal employed by the retail lawyer had written the pleadings. As Formal Op. 356 states:

> A client who retains a firm expects that the legal services will be rendered by lawyers and other personnel closely supervised by the firm. Client consent to the involvement of firm personnel and the disclosure to those personnel of confidential information necessary to the representation is inherent in the act of retaining the firm.

Regardless of who writes the pleadings, the retail lawyer bears full responsibility for the end product and is therefore entitled to all the credit (or blame).

Several state bar ethics committees have opined that if the wholesale lawyer will actually be representing the client in court, even on a minor motion, the retail lawyer must disclose this to the client beforehand and obtain the client's consent.[1] One state ethical opinion requires that such consent be obtained at the outset of the representation.[2]

The retail lawyer should be careful about showing a client's file or disclosing the client's confidences to a wholesale lawyer without the client's prior consent. Even if the ethics rules do not necessarily require such disclosure, a client might nevertheless be angry and file a grievance if the client were to learn that the retail lawyer revealed confidential information to a lawyer who was not a partner or associate in the retail lawyer's firm.

Confidentiality

Because the wholesale lawyer is so closely associated with the retail lawyer, it necessarily follows that the wholesale lawyer has the same duty of confidentiality regarding clients. It is extremely important for wholesale lawyers to uphold this duty of confidentiality, not only from the standpoint of avoiding disciplinary proceedings, but also so retail lawyers will trust them.

The wholesale lawyer may have, either in her files or in her brain, confidential information about hundreds of clients from a hundred law offices. She must be very careful not to discuss with one lawyer a case she is handling for another lawyer. There are exceptions, of course. For example, in cases where the opposition is aware that she is working on a case, she might discuss matters that are contained in public court papers relating to that case. Generally, though, retail lawyers (and their clients) have a right to expect that she will not discuss their matters with other lawyers (or nonlawyers, for that matter). A wholesale lawyer who speaks freely about particular matters she is handling for retail lawyers will quickly lose the confidence and trust of the retail lawyers who have hired her. A retail lawyer who hires a wholesaler knows that the wholesaler works for other retail lawyers as well, and will hire only a wholesaler he can fully trust not to divulge confidences.

In addition to the wholesale lawyer's duty of confidentiality to the retail lawyer's client, the wholesale lawyer owes a duty of confidentiality to the retail lawyer. Working as closely as she does with the retail lawyers who hire her, she knows their strengths, but she also knows their weaknesses. It is important that she not disclose these weaknesses to anyone. Retail lawyers hire her to help them look strong, not weak. The duty of confidentiality the wholesale lawyer owes personally to the retail lawyer may not be found in the Model Code or Rules of Professional Conduct, but it is a duty inherent in maintaining good business relations.

Conflicts of interest

Because the wholesale lawyer has the same duty of confidentiality that the retail lawyer has, the wholesale lawyer also has the same duty to avoid conflicts of interest. Conflicts of interest can arise frequently in wholesale law practice, particularly in smaller communities with fewer retail lawyers, because the fewer the retail lawyers, the greater the likelihood that two retail lawyers who are opposing each other will both seek the services of the same wholesale lawyer. An example: A wholesale lawyer has written a complaint for a plaintiff's lawyer. After the complaint is served on the defendant, defense counsel, unaware that the wholesale lawyer is working with plaintiff's counsel, requests the wholesale lawyer's services. This does not happen very often, but it happens often enough so that you should know how to respond in such a way that does not hurt the defendant's lawyer for inadvertently calling you.

The moment you determine that a lawyer is calling for help on a case in which you are already helping the other side, you should immediately tell the lawyer not to talk about it any further. If asked, you should disclose that you have a conflict, but you need not discuss the nature of the conflict. You can simply say, "I can't help you with this case because I have a conflict, but thanks for calling me, and please try me again another time."

What happens if a retail lawyer calls you for help on a case in which opposing counsel is also a retail lawyer for whom you work or have worked? If the subject matter of the two cases is substantially related, you may have a problem. In cases like this, the critical issue is whether confidential information gained in the first matter can be used against the former client in the second matter by the present client. However, so long as you do not breach the confidentiality of the former client, there probably will be no reason that prevents you from helping one retail lawyer customer against another retail lawyer you have served in the past. Under no circumstances, though, should a wholesale lawyer assist one retail lawyer in a case that is directly adverse to another lawyer's client (in effect, working for both sides).

The conflict-of-interest problem is probably not any worse for wholesale lawyers than it is for retail lawyers. For example, historically, labor and employment lawyers were exclusively on management's side or labor's side, but such exclusivity has diminished in recent years. Many large law firms that previously represented only employers are now representing employees as well. The same is true in debtor-creditor practice, domestic relations, personal injury law, and other areas.

Billing the client for the wholesale lawyer's work

If the retail lawyer charges the client a fixed fee or contingent fee, the client will not be billed for the wholesale lawyer's work (unless, of course, the retail lawyer and the client agree otherwise). If the client pays the retail lawyer an hourly fee, then the retail lawyer has two options: 1) bill the client separately for the wholesale lawyer's work as a disbursement; or 2) include the wholesale lawyer's hours in the retail lawyer's bill for professional services.

The vast majority of retail lawyers choose the latter. They simply bill the wholesale lawyer's hours at the retail lawyer's rate, in the same way that a law firm bills for an associate's time. Suppose an associate who bills 2,000 hours a year is paid a salary of $70,000. That means the firm is paying the associate $35 an hour. But the firm may be billing the client $150 an hour. It is none of the client's business what the firm pays the associate. If a law firm can charge $150 an hour for the work of an associate whom the firm pays $35 an hour, a retail lawyer can bill a client $150 an hour for the work of a wholesale lawyer whom the retail lawyer pays $35 an hour.

(Billing arrangements between wholesale lawyers and retail lawyers are covered in Chapter 5.)

Notes

1. *E.g., ABA/BNA Lawyers Man. on Prof. Conduct* §1001:5706 (*citing* N.H. Bar Ass'n Ethics Comm. Op. 1993–94/8)

2. *Ibid.* at §1001:3010 [*citing* Ill. St. Bar Ass'n Comm. on Professional Ethics, Op. 92–7 (1993)].

CHAPTER 4

Starting and Managing a Wholesale Law Practice: Questions and Answers

Is it feasible to maintain both a retail law practice and a wholesale law practice simultaneously?

Yes, with a few caveats. If you have a retail law practice and want to switch entirely to a wholesale law practice, financial necessity will probably compel you to maintain some of your retail practice while your wholesale practice gets up to speed. Of course, if you enjoy some aspects of retail practice, you might want to continue your retail practice indefinitely while also maintaining a part-time wholesale practice.

However, retail lawyers generally prefer to use wholesale lawyers who are not simultaneously competing with them for clients. Retail lawyers want to be sure that the wholesale lawyers they hire do not someday steal away clients.[1] Considering that the wholesale lawyer will usually get to meet the retail lawyer's client and might even work closely and regularly with the client, it is possible for a close, trusting relationship to develop between the wholesale lawyer and the client. A retail lawyer will feel used and betrayed if a wholesale lawyer exploits this situation by stealing the client. That is the cardinal sin of wholesale law practice.

You can be flexible. Your practice need not be 100 percent wholesale and 0 percent retail. It can be anywhere in between, and you can alter that ratio whenever you want. Even if you decide that you no longer wish to represent retail clients at all, there is nothing formal, final, or official about that decision. You need not take an oath to stay out of retail law practice, you need not surrender your license to practice law, and you need not announce to the world that you are no longer accepting retail clients. If a client comes along whom you wish to represent, you are always free to do so.

If I decide I no longer wish to represent retail clients, what should I do if one calls me?

If you have maintained a retail law practice, the general public will probably not know that you are no longer accepting retail clients, so you will probably continue to get calls from time to time from people who want you to represent them. If you don't wish to represent them, tell them you are no longer accepting new clients and refer them to one of the retail lawyers you serve. You may do the same with your existing clients or, at your option, continue to serve them. You should continue to handle existing cases, transactions, and other commitments you have already made, unless you and the clients mutually agree to your withdrawal. If you have clients who call you on a regular basis and you no longer wish to represent them, you should call them and tell them that they should no longer call you and that they should instead call one of the retail lawyers you recommend.

There is no need to tell *all* your existing and former clients that you have given up retail law practice. There is always the possibility that you will not enjoy, or will not succeed in, wholesale law practice, and will want to return to retail law practice. Don't burn any bridges unnecessarily.

As you develop a clientele of retail lawyers, make a list of their names and specialties and keep it handy so that if you do get calls from prospective retail clients, you can recommend them to one of the retail lawyers you serve. Don't tell the client, "I ghostwrite for Attorney X, give him a call." Just say, "I consult with Attorney X on cases; give him a call and tell him I recommended you to him." You might wish to call Attorney X yourself. There is no better way to keep retail lawyers happy than to refer cases to them. They might even ask you to work on these cases or, if the ethical rules in your jurisdiction permit, at least pay you a referral fee.

Must I specialize my wholesale law practice in one (or a few) areas of law?

Specialization is not a must, but it is highly desirable. A retail lawyer seeking the services of a wholesale lawyer in a particular case wants a wholesale lawyer who is an expert in the substantive and procedural aspects of that particular type of case, not simply a good researcher/writer. Retail lawyers do not want to pay hourly fees or large contingent fees to a wholesale lawyer who is learning from scratch.[2] You should specialize in one or a few areas of law and become a real expert in them. If your state has a certification procedure to become a "specialist," try to get certified, and highlight your certification when marketing yourself. You will be in greater demand that way.

The basic advantages and disadvantages of specialization are largely the same in wholesale law practice as they are in retail law practice. The advantages are 1) potential customers/clients are more apt to seek a specialist than a generalist; 2) a specialist can charge higher fees than a generalist can; and 3) a specialist can concentrate his or her mental energy into one or a few areas of law and be a master in those areas, rather than having to be a jack-of-all-trades, master of none.

The disadvantages of specialization are 1) specialists lose potential business and revenue in areas in which they do not specialize; 2) specialists run the risk that there will be insufficient demand for their specialty or an oversupply of lawyers with a similar specialty in their locale; 3) a specialty can be hot for a few years and then cool off or die due to legislative or economic changes; and 4) specialization can be boring to a lawyer who enjoys variety.

However, one factor particularly favors specialization in wholesale law practice: retail lawyers generally have a deeper understanding of the legal services the wholesale lawyer is providing than the retail clients have of the legal services the retail lawyer is providing. Thus, retail lawyers have a greater appreciation for, and demand for, specialists. Many retail clients are satisfied with a general practitioner. That is why, despite predictions over the years that they would become extinct, many general practitioners have continued to thrive. They are, perhaps, not quite as generalized as they once were. Few lawyers today are so generalized that they accept literally any client who walks in the door and can pay the fee. But as the lawyer listings in the Yellow Pages of any city telephone book attest, there are still many small-firm and solo lawyers who list six or eight disparate areas of law (e.g., criminal law, bankruptcy, real estate, divorce, personal injury, etc.) in which they practice, and many of these lawyers have large and successful practices. Their clients like them and have confidence in them for reasons other than, or in addition to, expertise alone. The retail lawyer, on the other hand, is concerned only about expertise and cost when hiring a wholesale lawyer. The retail lawyer is not looking for a psychological bond with the wholesale lawyer and does not need a wholesale lawyer with a tough persona or "connections," which is what retail clients often seek when hiring lawyers.

Specialization is, therefore, a virtual necessity in wholesale law practice. However, there are varying degrees of specialization. Law is not easily compartmentalized; it is a seamless web in which knowledge in one area is helpful in related areas. Thus, you can specialize without pigeonholing yourself too narrowly. You can overlap into some related areas if the opportunity arises.

How can I learn a specialty if I do not have one already?

First, think about the cases and transactions you have handled during your legal career, and decide which types of legal matters you enjoy most and have provided you with skills and knowledge that are marketable to other lawyers. Wholesale lawyers who specialize in cases and transactions that require much research and paperwork or that involve complex statutory or regulatory schemes are most in demand.

Next, buy some practice books or even law-school textbooks in those specialties and read them cover to cover, as though you were taking a course in their subject matter. In fact, you may consider taking either a CLE course or a course at a local law school (you can audit the course for a modest fee or, if you are a graduate of that school, possibly take it for free). If you are certain about the areas in which you want to specialize, buy a loose-leaf service for practitioners in those areas. Most loose-leaf services are payable on an installment basis, so they do not require much upfront capital.

Third, consider calling some lawyers who practice in that specialty and tell them you want to be a wholesale lawyer in that specialty but that you lack experience, and ask them if they would be willing to hire you in some minor capacity for a very low wage—even doing temporary, part-time secretarial or paralegal work—just so you can learn the nuts and bolts of practicing that specialty. Some might discourage you from entering their specialty, or from wholesaling in their specialty, but take their discouragement with a grain of salt. Some might worry that you are a potential competitor. You should reassure them that you are not a potential competitor, but rather a potential asset to them, because you want to help them represent their own clients, not take clients away from them. Others, however, will be delighted with your decision and will look forward to the day when you can help them.

If my suggestion that you consider doing secretarial or paralegal work shocks or offends you, remember that that is how I learned employment law. I am living proof that a lawyer can improve his career by getting off his high horse. The reason you should offer to do paralegal or secretarial work rather than be an associate is that small-firm lawyers probably need secretarial or paralegal assistance more than they need an associate. Also, hiring a secretary or paralegal is less expensive than hiring an associate, even at the same base pay. The associate needs an office, malpractice insurance, and perhaps some new equipment, whereas the secretary and paralegal can use existing space and facilities and need no malpractice insurance. Furthermore, if you tell these lawyers you want to be an associate, you might turn them off, for they will assume that you want a long-term relationship and, eventually, a much higher salary. By declaring your willingness to work as a secretary or paralegal, however, you prove to them that you just want to learn, that you are not relying too heavily on them for a living, and that you are not seeking any type of long-term relationship with them. That way, they will feel more comfortable about hiring you for a while. And who knows—maybe at some point down the road they will want you as an associate, or even a partner. But that should not be your goal right now, and you should not let them think that is your goal.

If no specialist in your immediate locale will hire you, call specialists fifty or seventy-five miles away (even if they are out of state; practicing a specialty out of state might not be too different from practicing it in your state). They will not regard you as potential competition, and they might jump at the opportunity to hire you. After all, where else can they find a real lawyer, as opposed to a nonlawyer secretary or paralegal, eager to learn their specialty and to help out with whatever needs to be done in the office—for *minimum wage!*

If no lawyer anywhere will hire you, call banks, insurance companies, corporations, construction companies, hospitals, accounting firms, supermarket chains, and other entities that regularly deal with the area of law you want to specialize in, and offer to do any type of work for them (again, for very low wages) that will enable you to gain practical experience in that specialty.

It takes great humility for a lawyer to ask another lawyer or a nonlawyer-manager, "Can I do your paperwork for $5.15 an hour?" Be prepared for some strange looks—and rejection. But remember, it takes only one such job offer to start you on the road to specialized wholesale law practice. Also remember that the key to landing such a position is your willingness to work for low wages. The lawyers and nonlawyers you approach will think you are a little odd, and no one wants to pay prevailing wage to an oddball. But for five bucks an hour or so, what have they got to lose?

You don't have to stay long. You can learn many practical skills in the course of three months or six months of hands-on experience in a specialized field. Many legal secretaries and paralegals learn more about probate, real estate, bankruptcy, incorporation procedures, and various other legal specialties in a short period of time than many unspecialized lawyers do over longer periods.

Then again, if you land a short-term job with a bank, insurance company, corporation, or other nonlegal employer, you might decide you want to stay there longer. As you become more familiar with the organization and its staff, you might take a liking to them—and they to you. If they are impressed with your ability and your attitude, they might offer you a better job—legal or nonlegal—opening up whole new career opportunities for you. These opportunities probably would not be available to you if you applied for them straight from your solo or small-firm law practice and were an unknown quantity to these organizations.

If no nonlegal employer will hire you, get together with other wholesale lawyers and organize a grass-roots movement to place lawyers in short-term (and possibly long-term) nonlegal and semilegal jobs in your community. [You will know who the other wholesale lawyers are because, as explained in Chapter 6, *infra*, you are going to help organize a "Legal Writers Section" or "Wholesale Lawyer Referral Service" within your state and/or local bar association.] Write to businesses, nonprofit organizations, and government agencies in your community, tell them about this group of lawyers (call yourselves "Lawyers for the Community" or some catchier name), and ask them to send job listings to the bar association. Maybe your Chamber of Commerce, United Way, and other umbrella organizations will help your group land such jobs. Let these employers and organizations know that this is not a marketing campaign or publicity stunt for lawyers, but rather a sincere effort by a group of lawyers to refocus their careers away from the combative type of lawyering that so many of these entities complain about. This is a genuine career move on their part. Some of these lawyers will then leave and go into wholesale law practice, using their new skills to help lawyers represent these organizations, while others will want to continue working for these organizations and quit law practice entirely. Let these organizations know that, according to numerous surveys,[3] at least one-third of all lawyers want to leave law practice and that these lawyers constitute a wealth of talent, experience, and character that can be mobilized to serve the nonlegal needs of these organizations.

Whatever you decide to do, you don't have to call yourself a "secretary" or "paralegal." If your new boss approves, call yourself a "consultant" or "consulting attorney" or "research counsel" or "project manager" or some other title that has more prestige than "secretary" or "paralegal." When I did paralegal work at Aetna, I called myself a "regulatory compliance analyst."

After you have learned enough about a specialty so that you feel confident offering wholesale legal services in that specialty, you can list in your announcements that you worked with Attorney So-and-So, or the Thus-and-Such Bank, on a long-term project, developed an intense interest in the subject matter, read a number of treatises on it, and are now ready, willing, and able to help other lawyers handle cases in that specialty.

Is it feasible for a recent law school graduate to start a wholesale law practice?

Because retail lawyers prefer specialized wholesale lawyers, wholesale law practice is more difficult for new lawyers to enter than it is for experienced lawyers. The new lawyer should consider working as an unpaid or low-paid intern, or a legal secretary or paralegal for a year or so during or after law school in an office that handles the types of cases in which he wishes to specialize. He will learn the substantive and procedural aspects of that specialty and then might be ready to open a wholesale law practice of his own. If he cannot land a regular job as a secretary, paralegal, or intern, he should tell some small-firm lawyers that he wants to fill in when their secretaries are on vacation, maternity leave, or sick leave. (He can also tell some large-firm lawyers, but large firms tend to be more traditional in their hiring practices and thus less apt to hire a lawyer as a secretary or paralegal.) As a legal secretary, he will quickly learn how to write basic legal documents as they are written in the various courts and agencies of his state. Many small-firm lawyers will be delighted to hire him because they know they are getting an intelligent, well-educated "temp" who is eager to learn legal procedures, and they don't have to pay a fee to an employment agency. For the lawyer's part, he should make sure he has taken whatever courses are necessary to learn the various types of software used in law firms.

After a few months, he might consider starting a freelance legal secretarial/paralegal service of his own. Small-firm lawyers, many of whom can use his help because they cannot afford to hire full-time legal assistants, will call him. When they see how talented he is, they will then give him some research/writing assignments, and before he knows it, he'll have a wholesale law practice of his own, perhaps even a specialized one.

There is some controversy over whether unemployed recent law school graduates should accept "low-status" jobs such as legal secretary or paralegal: How will it look on their resumes? Recent law grads, after all, need to be more concerned about their resumes than experienced wholesale lawyers do. Unlike experienced lawyers, they might not have the luxury of calling themselves something other than "secretary" or "paralegal." Experienced lawyers who choose wholesale law practice have, in many cases, given up sending out resumes or simply do not like retail law practice, and therefore have no reason to look for a job and send out resumes anymore. Recent law grads—most of whom, deep down, want to at least *try* retail law practice for a while—are more likely to try to use wholesale law practice as a stepping-stone to a job in retail law practice than experienced lawyers are, and therefore need to be careful about their resumes in this regard.

There are two schools of thought on this.[4] The traditional school holds that secretarial or paralegal work is "beneath" a lawyer and will look bad on his or her resume. But the current school is much more sympathetic to the plight of the average recent grad. Everyone in the legal community knows that legal jobs for new admittees are scarce and that many new admittees who are unemployed have great potential as retail or wholesale lawyers. A bright, eager, new admittee should not be expected to sit home cranking out cover letters and resumes *ad nauseum* when he or she has an opportunity to gain valuable legal experience doing secretarial or paralegal work. If you need inspiration, read "Post-Law School Job May Be as Paralegal" in the March 1995 *ABA Journal,* which shows a smiling 1978 graduate of a very good law school (Tulane) who has worked as a paralegal for 17 years.[5] If she can do it, you can do it. An October 1995 *Student Lawyer* article points out that "there are thousands of lawyers working as paralegals[.] There's even a new category in the classified section of the *New York Times:* 'Paralegal/J.D.' " This same commentator cautions that a firm that hires you as a paralegal might never respect you enough to promote you to an associate.[6] Even if that is true (it is probably true of some firms, but by no means all firms), that should not deter you from working there doing secretarial or paralegal work. After all, that firm was unwilling to hire you as an associate in the first place, which is why you are working there as a secretary or paralegal. So gain whatever experience you can there, make whatever contacts you can in the legal community (working at a law firm in any capacity will put you in contact with members of the legal community, inside and outside that firm), and either move on to another firm or start a wholesale or retail law practice of your own. If you are really talented, many firms will recognize your talent and give you more challenging work, such as legal research and drafting. Whether or not they offer you an associate's position, you will be better off in the long run than a less-talented recent grad who somehow managed to land a more prestigious first job.

Keep in mind that during the Great Depression, when jobs were scarce for everyone, many lawyers and other professionals worked part-time in low-prestige jobs to supplement their incomes. There has been enough publicity about the job scarcity for lawyers today so that no recent law grad should feel ashamed to accept low-prestige work.

Do I need an office outside my home?

You don't *need* an office outside your home, but it is highly desirable, even if it is very modest—say, a small, windowless room in a suite with other lawyers. It demonstrates your commitment and gives you a presence. If possible, rent an office in a downtown area as close as possible to as large a concentration of lawyers as exists in your locale. You will spend much time going to retail lawyers' offices to bring them documents you have written, to look at files you are working on, and to confer with them and their clients.

"Out of sight, out of mind" applies to wholesale law practice. A wholesale lawyer needs to continually remind the retail bar of his or her existence, availability, and eagerness to serve retail lawyers. Retail lawyers have a lot on their minds other than who the wholesalers are. Seeing you on the street or in the law library may remind them of a legal matter for which you might be of assistance. If they do not see you on the street or in the library, it might not occur to them to call you.

A very modest office is sufficient. Few lawyers will actually visit your office; they will want you to visit theirs. If you currently maintain a retail law practice, your present office will probably suffice for your wholesale law practice.

What equipment do I need?

You need two telephone lines and either an answering service or, preferably, a live receptionist. If you work strictly from your home, make sure you have business phone lines, not just residential phone lines, because business lines entitle you to a Yellow Pages listing (see Chapter 6 for a discussion of your Yellow Pages listing). The ideal situation is office-sharing with other lawyers, whose receptionist answers your phone.

You need a fax machine, a word processor or computer (try

to use software that is compatible with what many retail lawyers use, so you can easily transfer documents to them; however, it is usually acceptable to give them hard copy), and easy access to a good law library. This library need not be in your office; it can be near your office, perhaps in a courthouse or law school. If you are not near a courthouse or law school, consider talking to some lawyers near you and asking them if you can pay them a modest monthly fee to use their library.

Buy *The Bluebook* or whatever citation book your state uses. Read it carefully and use it often. You are holding yourself out as a legal research/writing expert. You must be meticulous, thorough, and totally up to date in your research and writing. Read *Lawyers Weekly* or whatever weekly newspaper summarizes new decisions and other legal developments in your state. Read advance sheets. Shepardize cases and statutes whenever you do legal research.

Whether you need computerized research capabilities is a matter of personal preference and financial ability, so you must decide that for yourself.

What if I am not a good legal writer?

Then become one! Any lawyer, even one of modest ability, can become a fine legal writer if he or she really wants to. All it takes is practice, a good teacher and/or tutor, and more practice.

Ask a law professor, retired judge, or some other lawyer with outstanding legal writing credentials (e.g., a former law review editor or former clerk to an appellate judge) to tutor you in legal writing, i.e., review and critique all the legal writing you do over the next few months, for an appropriate fee. When you show your writing to your tutor, redact party names and other information your clients would not want you to reveal.

Enroll in an advanced legal writing course at a local law school or CLE facility. Read some books on legal writing and legal citation. Proper citation is essential if you want to succeed as a wholesale lawyer. Read *The Bluebook*. If *The Bluebook* is too boring for you, read an article in a good academic law review on any topic of interest to you and pay careful attention to the footnotes. Notice the spacing, punctuation, and abbreviations in the citations; the use and wording of parentheticals following case cites; the use of "jump cites," i.e., citation to particular pages of a case or article;

the use of *see, see generally, cf.,* and other "signals"; and subsequent case histories. Good citation form is the hallmark of a good legal writer. It bespeaks the writer's intelligence, diligence, honesty, and respect for the court. It impresses judges, lawyers, clients, and adversaries alike.

Do I need to hire a legal assistant (secretary or paralegal)?

You will not spend all your time doing research and writing. You will spend much time printing, photocopying, faxing, filing, mailing, and delivering documents; talking on the phone with legal assistants about nontechnical matters such as deadlines, minor changes in documents, scheduling appointments, and the like; and paying your bills, putting advance sheets into binders, and keeping financial records. A good legal assistant can probably handle these tasks for you and perhaps be your marketing director as well, thus allowing you more time to use your specialized research/writing/consulting skills and take on more cases.

So the question for you is the same as it is for virtually all lawyers: Can you *afford* to hire a legal assistant? The analysis is the same for the wholesale lawyer as it is for the retail lawyer, except in two respects. First, because wholesale lawyers charge only a fraction of what retail lawyers charge, wholesale law practice is viable only if the wholesaler's overhead is low, and it is difficult to keep overhead low if one hires a legal assistant.

Second, the retail lawyer who asks you to help her on a case probably already has a legal assistant. If that retail lawyer felt that her legal assistant were capable of doing the work the retail lawyer asked you to do, the retail lawyer would not have called you. The retail lawyer called you because you are an expert in *all* aspects of handling that particular case, including the ministerial aspects. That is why, as Appendix B indicates, many retail lawyers insist that the wholesale lawyer not delegate responsibilities.[7] Wholesale lawyers are permitted little margin for error. They are hired to do precise work, and they must do it precisely. That often means they must do it themselves. They must be legal experts and legal assistants rolled into one.

Speaking of legal assistants, it is important that you develop excellent working relationships with the legal assistants who work for the retail lawyers you serve. If you are pressed for time, they will often help you. They might pick up a document from your office if you are too busy to bring it to them. They might prepare a simple motion that you otherwise would be expected to prepare. Cooperation between you and the office staffs of retail lawyers can eliminate the need for you to hire a staff of your own, and will enable you to keep your fees lower, which retail lawyers will appreciate.

Do I need malpractice insurance?

Yes. Obviously, if you maintain a retail law practice in addition to your wholesale law practice, you should carry malpractice insurance. If you maintain only a wholesale practice, you should still carry malpractice insurance. You will meet and talk to most of the clients whose cases you work on, and if a client were to sue the retail lawyer who hired you, the client would probably sue you as well.

Malpractice insurance can be expensive. Tell your insurer how much of your practice consists merely of doing research and writing for other lawyers and how rarely you file appearances in their cases. The insurer might give you a discount on your premium or some kind of a credit for being a "part-time" lawyer.

Do I need a docket control system?

Yes, not so much to avoid malpractice, but to serve retail lawyers better. Theoretically, a wholesale lawyer can handle a much larger caseload than a retail lawyer can. A retail lawyer spends much more time with clients and adversaries than a wholesale lawyer does and is responsible for *every* aspect of a case, from initial client interview to settlement negotiations to trial to postjudgment proceedings. So a retail lawyer can handle only about half (a very rough estimate) as many cases as can a wholesale lawyer, who is handling only parts of each case. The larger your caseload, the greater the need for a docket control system. Of course, the wholesale lawyer is not the one who is *ultimately* responsible for meeting deadlines. That is the retail lawyer's responsibility, insofar as it is the retail lawyer who will have to answer to the court and the client if a deadline is missed. However, the retail lawyer in turn relies on the wholesale lawyer to make sure that deadlines are met.

When a retail lawyer you are working with receives a set of

interrogatories that must be answered within forty-five days, or a court's scheduling order requiring that summary judgment motions be filed by a certain date, the retail lawyer should inform you immediately. The retail lawyer should maintain his or her own docket control system, of course, but you should also keep a record of these deadlines so you can arrange your schedule and remind the retail lawyer of these deadlines.

Can a lawyer in a large law firm provide wholesale legal services to solo and small-firm lawyers?

Yes. There is no reason wholesale lawyers have to be solo or small-firm lawyers. Whether it makes economic sense for the large firm is hard to say.

The large-firm wholesale lawyer would certainly have to assure the small-firm retail lawyer that the large firm will not "steal" the client away.

If a wholesale lawyer spends most of the time working with just two or three different retail lawyers, is it advisable to be listed as "of counsel" on their letterheads?

A lawyer who is officially "of counsel" to a retail lawyer is not really a wholesale lawyer at all, at least with respect to that particular retail lawyer.[8]

Functionally, however, a wholesale lawyer is similar to an "of counsel." Certainly the "of counsel" designation has more prestige than "wholesale lawyer," "contract lawyer," "temp," or whatever term is used to describe freelancers. And, according to *ABA Formal Opinion 357,* a lawyer is ethically permitted to be of counsel to more than one lawyer or firm. So why not be on the letterhead?

The major disadvantage is that other retail lawyers might be less inclined to seek your services. They might assume that, because you are so closely associated with those lawyers on whose letterheads you appear, you might be inclined to steer clients towards those lawyers. As mentioned at the beginning of this chapter, retail lawyers will be disinclined to use wholesale lawyers who pose a risk of stealing clients. If you have no interest in expanding your wholesale law practice, then you might be better off with the more prestigious "of counsel" designation. But if you do want to expand, you are better off being on no one's letterhead but your own.

Notes

1. *See* Robin Page West, "Choosing Co-counsel," 10 *Compleat Lawyer* 16, 18 (Fall 1993) ("Some attorneys are reluctant to work with co-counsel because they fear co-counsel will steal their clients.").

2. "A New Class of Lawyers: Contract Workers," 12 *Compleat Lawyer* 5 (Fall 1995) (opinion of contract lawyer John Wallace); *see also* Joel P. Bennett, "Leveraging Your Practice with Independent Contractor Attorneys," *Law Prac. Mgmt.*, July/Aug. 1995, at 32 ("experienced independent contractor attorneys work better in my kind of practice than law students"); Sandra Goldsmith, "Briefly" ("The Temping Option"), 23 *Student Lawyer* 4 (May 1995) (recent law school graduates usually cannot be placed as temporary attorneys but can be placed as paralegals, according to Shelley Wallace of Wallace Law Registry).

3. *See* Mary Ann Glendon, *A Nation Under Lawyers* 85 (New York: Farrar, Straus and Giroux 1994) (gathering survey results).

4. Hope Viner Samborn, "Post-Law School Job May Be as Paralegal," 81 *A.B.A. J.* 14, 15 (Mar. 1995).

5. *Ibid.*

6. Ron Coleman, "Go Home," 24 *Student Lawyer* 30, 32 (Oct. 1995).

7. *See* page 111 *infra* (Short-form contingent fee agreement); *cf.* D.M. Osborne, "Should You Be Afraid of This Man?" *Am. Lawyer,* June 1995, at 74 (discussing the concern of a customer of a national legal research firm that the research will be done by a law student rather than an "expert").

8. ABA Formal Opinion 356.

CHAPTER 5

Setting and Collecting Fees

Hourly fees, fixed fees, contingent fees, and creative fee alternatives

Fee-setting in wholesale law practice is much the same as it is in retail law practice, except that the dollar amounts are obviously lower. Wholesale lawyers charge retail lawyers hourly fees, fixed fees, contingent fees, and combinations thereof (for example, a low hourly fee plus a low percentage of the retail lawyer's fee). Discounts to preferred customers (for example, retail lawyers who account for a significant percentage of the wholesale lawyer's revenue or who pay the wholesale lawyer immediately) are common and expected. Creative fee arrangements such as "incentive billing," "value billing," and other "share the pain, share the gain"[1] types of fee arrangements are welcome and sometimes even demanded.

Most retail lawyers want to pay the wholesale lawyer the same type of fee the retail lawyer is receiving from the client in that particular case. So if the retail lawyer is charging the client an hourly fee, the retail lawyer wants to pay the wholesale lawyer an hourly fee. This does not necessarily mean that the retail lawyer needs to tell the wholesale lawyer what type of fee the retail lawyer is charging, nor does it mean that the wholesale lawyer should ask. What the retail lawyer charges the client is none of the wholesale lawyer's business unless the retail lawyer is paying the wholesale lawyer a contingent fee. Usually, however, the wholesale lawyer will have the knowledge and experience in her specialty to be able to figure out what type of fee (if not the actual *amount* of the fee or hourly rate) the retail lawyer is charging in a case without having to ask the retail lawyer.

For example, transactional work is generally done on an hourly-fee or fixed-fee basis, litigation defense is nearly always done on an hourly-fee basis, domestic relations work is about evenly divided between hourly and flat fees, plaintiff's personal injury work is nearly always done on a contingent-fee basis, other types of plaintiff's litigation is usually done on a contingent-fee or mixed basis (i.e., contingent fee plus a retainer which is chargeable towards the contingent fee), and criminal defense is usually done on a fixed-fee basis.

The wholesale lawyer should have a base hourly rate that he or she is willing to accept, regardless of how the retail lawyer is charging the client. So if a retail lawyer calls you and asks how much you charge, you can respond, "I charge X dollars an hour" [the "X" will be discussed in a moment]. Feel free to go lower than X if you wish, just as retail lawyers vary their hourly rates depending on who the client is, what type of case it is, and what type of month they are having. But be careful—if you charge Lawyer A $30 an hour and Lawyer B $50 an hour, and your name comes up when Lawyer A is having lunch with Lawyer B, Lawyer B might learn that you charge him more and might be upset about that. On the other hand, you should not hesitate to give Lawyer A a break if he has a case you really want to work on, or has fallen on hard times, or is new to practice. Retail lawyers give breaks to clients, so wholesale lawyers can give breaks to retail lawyers.

If you think the retail lawyer might be charging her client a contingent fee, you should say something like this:

> I charge forty dollars an hour, but I might be willing to go lower or even charge no hourly fee if, one, you want to pay me a contingent fee, *if you* earn a fee; and, two, I decide, after taking an initial look at the case and talking to you and your client together, that there is a good potential for a substantial recovery in the case.

Most retail lawyers will want to pay you a contingent fee if they are being paid a contingent fee in the case. You will be amazed at how many lawyers who represent plaintiffs in litigation are unwilling to pay you even $25 an hour but will gladly pay you one-third of their fee in the case even if their fee turns out to be a million dollars. These lawyers simply do not want to pay money out of their pockets unless and until they receive money in the case. That is the very nature of a contingent fee. Although the standard justification for contingent fees is that they enable people with no money to obtain counsel, the fact is that many plaintiffs in tort cases do have some money they could pay a lawyer but nevertheless prefer to pay (and their lawyers prefer to receive) contingent fees. Even well-to-do plaintiffs in tort cases and many other types of litigation are ordinarily charged contingent fees. Similarly, even retail lawyers who have lots of money usually prefer to pay the wholesale lawyer a contingent fee if the retail lawyer is receiving a contingent fee.

So the question is rarely whether a plaintiff's lawyer wants to pay you a contingent fee (they nearly always do), but rather whether you want to accept a contingent fee. Are you willing to spend tens or even hundreds of hours on a case which, if it loses, will pay you nothing? Your answer should be: It depends on the case. Plaintiffs' lawyers do it all the time. Remember, however, that the plaintiffs' lawyer who uses a wholesale lawyer will not be doing all the work herself, but rather will expect the wholesale lawyer to do much of the work. If you are hesitant about taking a case on a straight contingent fee basis (i.e., you make nothing if the retail lawyer makes nothing), then offer the retail lawyer a compromise: say, $20 an hour plus 20 percent of the retail lawyer's fee; or offer the retail lawyer your standard hourly rate—say, $40 an hour—up to, say, 20 hours, and after the retail lawyer has paid you $800, then your fee is 25 percent of the lawyer's fee.

The effective use of contingent fees can generate a sizable income for a wholesale lawyer, just as it can for a retail lawyer. The same risk-vs.-return principle applies to both. As explained in Chapter 4, a wholesale lawyer can handle a much larger caseload than a retail lawyer can because a wholesale lawyer handles only parts of cases. A wholesale lawyer can own a piece of dozens and dozens of cases from many different retail lawyers and make much more than she can charging $40 an hour. On the other hand, if a wholesale lawyer is careless and agrees to work on a contingent-fee basis in many cases which eventually lose, she will earn little. Retail lawyers will take advantage of her. They will accept cases they know are weak, then dump the work on their good-natured wholesale lawyer hoping she turns a few of them into winners. She will be overworked and underpaid.

Wholesale lawyers just starting out need to be especially cautious about accepting contingent-fee work because even the good cases often take a few years to settle or go to trial. The new wholesale lawyer should try to get paid by the hour to the extent necessary to meet current expenses, and take a few contingent-fee cases which might pay off in the future.

If the wholesale lawyer agrees to work on a contingent-fee basis, and the retail lawyer is being paid one-third of the recovery in the case, the wholesale lawyer should ordinarily be paid one-third of the retail lawyer's fee, that is, one-ninth of the recovery. So if a case settles for $90,000, the client gets $60,000, the wholesale lawyer gets $10,000, and the retail lawyer keeps $20,000.

Some retail lawyers will not agree to pay you a third of their third. They will only want to pay you one-fourth or as little as one-fifth. Some retail lawyers will agree to pay you one-third of their fee, but they are only charging the client one-fourth of the recovery. Be prepared to do some bargaining with retail lawyers at the outset of the case in these situations. There is no hard-and-fast guidance on this. You must determine, on a case-by-case basis, the percentage you are willing to accept, taking into consideration 1) how much work you will have to do, 2) how strong the case is and how high the potential recovery is, and 3) how capable the retail lawyer is. Obviously, you are better off agreeing to one-fourth of a truly superb retail lawyer's fee in a strong, high-stakes case than one-third of a mediocre retail lawyer's fee in a weak, low-stakes case.

Sometimes a plaintiff's lawyer will be unwilling to pay you a third or a quarter of her fee because she only needs limited service from you in a case. She just wants you to write a brief or a motion once in a while, or wants advice from you occasionally, or wants you to cover for her at a deposition. You should offer to do this work at your standard hourly rate, but you might also wish to suggest a small contingent fee (say, 10 percent of the retail lawyer's fee).

Sometimes a lawyer will call you to ask if you already have a brief on a particular topic. If you do, sell her the brief for a price you think is fair. In most instances, you do not need permission from the lawyer for whom you initially wrote that brief, especially if the brief is a matter of public record, i.e., it is on public file in a courthouse, which means you are not revealing the confidences of a client. If the brief is a matter of public record, and the retail lawyer asks you, "Can you give me the case name and number so I can look up that brief in the courthouse and photocopy it?", feel free to decline. You are entitled to charge for that brief, even though someone else already paid you for it and even though the retail lawyer, if he knew the case name or number, could find it himself and photocopy it. It is accepted practice and is no different than a real estate lawyer selling a title abstract she did a few years ago. You are in the business of helping lawyers represent their clients, and because you are, you are entitled to be paid for helping retail lawyers. This retail lawyer would have had to spend much time researching and writing a brief himself, so he should pay you something for saving him that time even if it took you little time to do so. Of course, this is not to suggest that you should always charge for your service. You should provide free service on occasion, just as retail lawyers do.

What should your hourly rate be?

As a rule of thumb, your hourly rate should be about 30 percent of the true hourly rate of the average small-firm retail lawyer in your area. The true hourly rate is the rate retail lawyers are routinely charging and collecting from most of their clients, not what they boast about charging. If you ask the average small-firm retail lawyer what he charges, he might say "$175 an hour." But in fact he might collect $175 an hour only from a handful of clients, and collect only $100 an hour (or less) from most of his clients. Here in western Massachusetts, where the economy has been in a recession for the last five years and there are quite a few lawyers (Springfield is within 150 miles of twenty-five law schools, including some very large and prestigious ones), many lawyers have little cash to pay a wholesale lawyer. Retail lawyers here are willing and able to pay between $25 an hour and $45 an hour, and they expect a discount after a certain number (say, twenty) of hours. Large-firm retail lawyers can pay more, but large-firm retail lawyers rarely use wholesale lawyers; their associates do the wholesale work. Your hourly rate will thus depend on the economy of your region; whether you are in a large city, small city, or rural area; your specialty; and your reputation for quality and dependability. You might be able to charge more for rush jobs, but keep in mind that most lawyers will be rushing you all the time and may not want to pay premium rates for the privilege. They will expect you to do quality work, in a rush, all the time. Wholesale lawyers face constant deadline pressure, and the wholesale lawyer who is always asking for an extension will have difficulty attracting business.

Because most wholesale lawyers depend mainly on small-firm retail lawyers for business, few wholesale lawyers will be able to charge more than about $60 an hour, in any market, in the mid-1990s. The norm will be $30 to $45 an hour. However, you might be able to charge, say, $60 an hour for the first five hours, then reduce it to $35 an hour. You might wish to ask some other wholesale lawyers in your area what they charge, but don't believe everything you hear. Boasting about fees and income is common in law and other status-conscious professions. When other wholesale lawyers tell you that their true rate (what they generally charge and collect) is $65 or $85 an hour, be skeptical. Maybe they are telling you the truth, maybe they aren't.

When does the wholesale lawyer get paid?

Having read this chapter so far, you are probably worried that the answer to this question is "When the retail lawyer gets paid." Well, yes and no. When you work on a contingent-fee basis, you get paid when the retail lawyer gets paid. When you work on a fixed-fee basis, you submit a bill to the retail lawyer when your work is done (although some retail lawyers will pay you the fixed amount even without receiving a bill). When you work on an hourly-fee basis, you submit a bill periodically or when your work is done. Upon receipt of your bill, the retail lawyer will pay you either immediately or when he pays his other bills (in a few days, a few weeks, a few months [after you have rebilled him a few times], or when he next needs your services). You would obviously prefer to get paid on the spot, i.e., when you submit your bill, but most retail lawyers will prefer to pay your bill at their convenience.

You must approach this issue the way any businessperson

does. If you insist on immediate payment from everyone, some will oblige, but others might take their business elsewhere. You might wish to discuss this with the retail lawyers you serve. Ask them if they are willing to pay you immediately upon receipt of your bill, and if they are, offer them a lower hourly rate. Try not to look desperate. Don't appear as though you will starve if you don't get paid immediately; they might assume that your poverty results from ineptitude.

But feel free to tell a few retail lawyers (perhaps the ones with whom you are close friends) that you will give them low rates indefinitely if they pay you on the spot. When I started my wholesale law practice, most of the lawyers who called me were representing plaintiffs on a straight contingent-fee basis (no retainer) and thus wanted to pay me a straight contingent fee. But there was one plaintiff's lawyer who was willing to pay me $25 an hour plus 15 percent of his fee, if any. He had several big cases and needed about twenty hours a week from me for several months. Because I greatly appreciated and needed the $500 (or so) a week he was paying me, I spent more than twenty hours a week on these cases and put in a maximum effort to make sure that my work was superb—but I did not charge him for these extra hours. Whenever I brought him documents, he paid me on the spot, before he even read the documents. Without him, I'm not sure I would have survived my first few months in wholesale law practice. I remain grateful to him to this day, so I still charge him only $25 an hour even though my standard hourly rate for other retail lawyers is now $35 to $40 an hour. Try to find a few retail lawyers like him if you are short of cash.

Should you ask a retail lawyer for a retainer? That is up to you. I don't ask for retainers, but you might feel differently.

The bottom line

With a good mix of hourly and contingent fees, a hard-working, specialized wholesale lawyer should be able to earn a decent living. Here's how it adds up.

Suppose a lawyer is in his fourth year of wholesale law practice. He rents an office in a modest suite with two other lawyers. His rent is $500 a month, which includes free use of the photocopier, fax machine, and law library (consisting only of the state statutes). His telephone is answered at no charge by the other lawyers' secretary. He has no secretary; he does all his own secretarial work. He owns his office computer and has another computer at home. He uses the courthouse law library a few blocks away.

He spends most of his time helping retail lawyers handle litigation, half for plaintiffs, half for defendants. Let us assume, for simplicity's sake, that in plaintiffs' cases, he charges either $35 an hour or one-third of the retail lawyer's fee; in defense cases he charges $35 an hour. He has a few clients of his own, whom he charges $120 an hour. He spends about three hours a day working on the $35-an-hour cases, a half hour a day working on the $120-an-hour cases, and the rest of his time on the contingent-fee cases.

Over the course of the year, six of the plaintiffs' cases win or settle for about $30,000 each. Thus his income from those cases is one-ninth of $180,000, or $20,000. Another plaintiff's case settles for $90,000, so his income from that case is $10,000.

Here is what his income statement for that year might look like:

REVENUES		
Hourly fees—$35 an hour		
$35 × 3 hour/day × 250 days		$26,250
Hourly fees—$120 an hour		
$120 × .5 hour/day × 250 days		15,000
Six contingent-fee cases totaling $180,000 in proceeds		
1/9 × $180,000		20,000
One contingent-fee case totaling $90,000 in proceeds		
1/9 × $90,000		10,000
Total Revenue		$71,250
EXPENSES		
Rent		$6,000
Office supplies		500
CLE		500
Advertising		
Ad in lawyers newspaper	800	
Martindale-Hubbell	1,000	1,800
Malpractice insurance		2,000
Telephone		
Two phone lines, long-distance calls, 1/2-inch ad in Yellow Pages		2,000
Publications		
Lawyers newspaper	250	
Loose-leaf service	750	
Books	500	1,500

Bar association dues	
County, state, ABA, and one specialized bar	700
Entertainment	
Holiday party for lawyers, taking lawyers to lunch, etc.	1,000
Total Expenses	$16,000
TOTAL INCOME	$55,250

Should your fee agreements be in writing?

This is a matter of personal preference and style. Most of the retail lawyers with whom I work are personal friends of mine, so I do not ask them to enter into written fee agreements with me. Maybe someday I'll get stiffed, but I haven't yet. Lawyers will be more inclined to hire you if you show them you trust them, and might feel insulted if you show distrust by asking them to sign fee agreements. Despite all the lawyer jokes, the fact remains that no other profession has such high ethical requirements to enter and stay in the profession as the legal profession does, so I trust lawyers to honor their oral agreements with other lawyers. You might feel differently.

Sometimes it is the retail lawyer who wants a written fee agreement, in which case you should oblige. But if a retail lawyer does not ask me for a written fee agreement, I generally do not ask for one. In hourly fee cases, I send out periodic bills. If a lawyer were to stiff me, I would simply stop working for that lawyer. In all honesty, however, my collection rate is 100 percent (although some lawyers pay very slowly).

Be particular about with whom you work on a contingent-fee basis. If a lawyer you've never met or heard of before asks you to work on a case on a straight contingent basis, you should probably (though not necessarily) decline. A straight contingent fee is risky for you because you can end up doing a lot of work for nothing (of course, the same can happen to the retail lawyer). Generally speaking, you should agree to it only if the case is quite promising and you either know the retail lawyer well or the retail lawyer is fairly prominent in your legal community. If you know a lawyer well, or the lawyer is prominent, you can probably trust that lawyer enough not to ask for a written fee agreement, even in a contingent-fee case, but this is an issue you really must decide for yourself on a case-by-case basis; I cannot tell you who to trust.

If you do use a written contingent-fee agreement, there's one issue you might wish to consider, depending on how cynical you are: Should you include a provision requiring the retail lawyer, upon receiving the recovery proceeds in the case, to show you the release or the proceeds check or some other proof of the recovery amount? Suppose you work on a case on a contingent basis where you are to receive one-third of the retail lawyer's fee, and the retail lawyer calls you and says, "I settled that case for $27,000; the client gets $18,000, I get $6,000, and you get $3,000; your check is in the mail; thanks for your help." How do you know the case settled for $27,000? What if it settled for $270,000? Once again, I trust lawyers not to cheat me, so I do not ask for confirmation. But you might feel differently. Just remember that if, at the outset of a case, you do insist on such a provision in your contingent-fee agreement with a retail lawyer, that retail lawyer might be so offended by your insinuation that he might take his business elsewhere.

Keep in mind that a contract binds both parties: the retail lawyer *and* the wholesale lawyer. While writing this book, I fell behind on a few projects I was working on for retail lawyers, and I asked some of them to perform tasks that I otherwise would have performed. If I had sought to bind these lawyers by having them sign contracts at the outset of our relationship, they might have bound *me* to these contracts. But because I have always been flexible with them, they were flexible with me.

Also keep in mind that preparing written fee agreements is time consuming and can be a drag on a high-volume, fast-turnaround, top-quality wholesale law practice. If a lawyer calls you and needs a brief for next Monday, you should not be wasting your time putting together a fee agreement and wasting her time having to read it and possibly haggle with you over it. A form agreement might work in a pinch, but there are so many different possible working arrangements between wholesale and retail lawyers that a one-size-fits-all form will rarely suffice. If a lawyer you have never heard of offers you an assignment requiring sixty hours of your time, perhaps you should have a written fee agreement, and maybe even a retainer. But most jobs take fewer than sixty hours, and the more time you spend on the fee agreement, the lower your profit margin. Also, believe it or not, many lawyers—retail and wholesale—do not like to sign things. You might even be one of them.

Do what is best for you. If you do not use written fee agreements or engagement letters, you should at least protect yourself by making contemporaneous notes to yourself that detail your oral agreements with retail lawyers.

Some short form sample fee agreements appear in Appendix B. You may wish to add provisions of your own.[2]

Notes

1. *See* Dick Dahl, "Share the Pain, Share the Gain," 82 *A.B.A.J.* 68 (June 1996); *See also* Richard C. Reed, *Billing Innovations: New Win-Win Ways to End Hourly Billing* (Chicago: ABA 1996).

2. Some sample provisions appear in Samuel A. Frederick, "Controlling Costs by Using Temporary Attorneys," *Law Practice Management* July/August 1995, at 36–40; Joel P. Bennett, "Leveraging Your Practice with Independent Contractor Attorneys," id. at 32; and Kathryn S. Marshall, "The Contract Lawyer," Law Office Economics & Management Manual § 11.07 (Dearfield, IL: Clark Boardmon Callahan 1995 Supp.).

CHAPTER 6

Marketing a Wholesale Law Practice

Marketing a wholesale law practice is remarkably similar to marketing a retail law practice.

Send letters or brochures

Begin by sending a letter or brochure to every small-firm lawyer you know, and also to some lawyers you know in large and medium-sized firms and some lawyers you don't know but who you think might be interested in your legal research/writing/consulting service. Tell them about your service and the flexible fee arrangements (hourly, contingent, fixed, and mixed fees) you offer. Offer them an introductory free hour of service. Tell them you do not charge for short phone calls (less than twenty minutes). Schedule an open house at your office, invite these lawyers to it, and, if you are really ambitious, follow up your invitation by calling them.

Send letters and brochures also to small in-house corporate legal departments. They are listed alphabetically and by state in the *Directory of Corporate Counsel,* which is available in most law libraries. Also send a mailing to small municipal legal departments. They are usually listed in a directory available in your library or even in your own *Lawyers Diary and Manual* or other such publication. These small legal departments often do not have enough lawyers to do all the research and writing they need.

Send these mailings periodically, not just once. It is better to send a letter or brochure to 100 lawyers four times a year than to send it to 400 lawyers once. A letter or brochure mailed once to 400 lawyers will be forgotten by the vast majority of them within minutes. But if you send the same, or a similar, mailing every few months, it will register in their minds.

Join

Join the sections of the ABA and of your state and local bar associations that pertain to your areas of practice and become active in these sections. Become a leader in these areas of practice. Most state bar associations will, on request, either give you or sell you a list of all section members. Write to all section members to offer them your service. Tell them what your qualifications are. Consider getting a toll-free number so that lawyers in other parts of your state can call you without paying long-distance charges. Offer to visit them if they are not too far away and, if you can afford it, buy them lunch.

Your Yellow Pages listing

You should be listed in the lawyer section of the Yellow Pages even if you have no retail clients. Although few if any lawyers will look to the Yellow Pages to decide which wholesale lawyer to use, they might use it to find your address and phone number. If they don't see your name there, they might not call you.

You do not need a display ad in the Yellow Pages, but if you do have one (perhaps for your retail law practice), you have a difficult decision to make: Should your listing indicate that you provide services to other lawyers? *Mainly* to other lawyers? *Solely* to other lawyers? The more you demonstrate to the legal community that you concentrate on serving lawyers rather than clients, the more retail lawyers will call you. However, should you decide that you don't like wholesale law practice or that you need to maintain a retail law practice part-time in order to supplement your income in wholesale law practice, you have a problem: an ad that states that you mainly or solely work for other lawyers will deter nonlawyer clients from calling you. They will assume that you only want to work for lawyers. And, unlike many other types of advertisements, the Yellow Pages last a whole year. You cannot change your Yellow Pages ad until a new phone book comes out. Thus, unless you are firmly and exclusively committed to wholesale law practice, you should probably err on the side of caution and either not list your research/writing service or list it in addition to the retail legal services you provide in your ad.

Your letterhead and business card(s)

You might want to have two sets of letterhead and business cards: one for lawyers, that indicates that you do legal research and writing for other lawyers and what your specialty (if any) is; and the other for your retail law practice (if any) and general purposes.

Advertise

If you can afford it, advertise your research/writing/consulting service in *Lawyers Weekly* or whatever weekly lawyers newspaper you receive. You might also be able to advertise in your state and local bar association newsletters. If you can afford it, buy an ad in *Martindale-Hubbell* highlighting your academic and professional accomplishments. A client in a slip-and-fall case might not care whether his lawyer is book-smart, but his lawyer definitely wants a wholesale lawyer who is book-smart. The wholesale lawyers who project the most scholarly image will be the ones most in demand. If you went to one of the better-rated law schools, or graduated cum laude, or won an *AmJur* award, or made law review, or wrote a scholarly article, buy a *Martindale-Hubbell* ad. That's the first place retail lawyers look to check out their wholesalers' credentials.

If you cannot afford a *Martindale-Hubbell* ad, make sure that you are at least listed in the *Martindale-Hubbell* blue pages and in all other lawyer directories in your state that provide free listings. If lawyers are contemplating calling you for help but don't see your name listed in the standard lawyer directories, they might wonder if you are really a member of the bar.

Write articles and speak at seminars

Write articles! Most bar associations have section newsletters and are always looking for articles to publish; you might also write an article for your weekly lawyers newspaper. These articles make good enclosures when you send mailings to lawyers. Better yet, write your own newsletter for lawyers. Be a seminar panelist.

Go wherever lawyers go

Participate in every bar association dinner, walkathon, golf outing, dial-a-lawyer service, etc., that you can. Wherever lawyers gather, that's where you should be, with plenty of business cards.

In-person solicitation of retail lawyers

When marketing your services to retail lawyers, you are not bound by the solicitation rules which govern your marketing to retail, nonlawyer clients. You can offer assistance to any lawyer at any time in any (reasonable) manner. You can even cold-call lawyers.

One place you might go to solicit lawyers—but you must be very discreet, quiet, and unintrusive—is the law library of your local courthouse. Don't go table to table handing out business cards and brochures as though you were running for office. But when you are in the law library, look around to see who is there. Obviously, every lawyer there is working on some kind of research project, and some of these lawyers will look lost or frustrated. They might ask silly questions of the librarians. (We who love legal research often forget that many lawyers hate it.) If you can do so *very discreetly,* offer your assistance to a lawyer who is having difficulty. Don't say, "Hi, I can tell you have no idea what you are doing, so I'd like to help you; I charge thirty-five dollars an hour; here's my card." Don't even mention, at least at first, that you do legal research and writing for a living. After you have helped the lawyer, give him or her your business card.

Even if you choose not to solicit lawyers in the law library, make a list of the lawyers you see there often and write to them to offer your service. You might also wish to call or visit some law librarians in courthouses around your state and ask them who their frequent lawyer-patrons are. If they tell you, you should write to these lawyers as well.

Of course, your mere presence in the law library is a good marketing tool. When lawyers see you there often, they will assume that you are a good legal researcher and that you are getting work from other lawyers. They will ask you questions and might follow up with a call for your services.

But don't be a pest. Don't solicit in the law library often. Do it once in a while—carefully. Lawyers go there to work, not to be bothered.

Monitor new and pending cases in your local courthouse

While you are in the courthouse, check out the docket of pending and newly-filed cases. If you see a case you would like to work on and which is being handled by a small-firm lawyer, call that lawyer and offer your service.

Greet new small law firms

When you read your weekly lawyers newspaper, read the announcements for new law firms. When you see an announcement for a new one-person or small firm, write to the lawyer listed and offer your services, especially if the announcement lists a field of practice in which you have some expertise.

Consider using a trade name

Consider using a trade name for your wholesale law practice, especially if you limit your practice to one area of law. Call yourself "Smith's Tort Litigation Services" or "Deborah Jones Commercial Law Research Center." Most states have ethical rules governing your use of a trade name when dealing with the general public, but not when dealing exclusively with your fellow lawyers. Thus, if you maintain a retail law practice in addition to your wholesale law practice, you might need one set of letterhead for your wholesale practice (using the trade name) and another set for your retail practice ("Deborah Jones, Attorney at Law"), depending on the rules in your jurisdiction. Using a trade name in your wholesale practice demonstrates your commitment to wholesale legal services and your keen interest in one area of law—and can be an effective eye-catcher.

Entertain

Hold a holiday party in December and invite all the retail lawyers who use your services, as well as some potential users. If you do not send formal, written invitations, then supplement your holiday effort by sending them holiday greeting cards as well. And don't hesitate to throw parties for lawyers at other times of the year, too. For example, if your office has a good view of the fireworks, hold a Fourth of July party!

On occasion, offer "satisfaction guaranteed"

Not all retail lawyers who call you have made a firm decision to hire you. Many want more information about you and perhaps about wholesale legal services generally—they want to "kick the tires." If a retail lawyer is hesitant, you might be able to close the deal by offering "satisfaction guaranteed": if the retail lawyer is not satisfied with your work, he doesn't have to pay you for it.

You might also use this approach to persuade a retail lawyer to give you greater responsibility than she had originally planned. Let me give you an example. A prominent Boston lawyer called me for help on a summary judgment motion involving, she said, three legal issues. The three issues had been researched and briefed by three different law student interns in her firm. She asked me to edit the three briefs and blend them together into a coherent whole. I estimated that my total fee, at $35 an hour, would be about $350, and she gave the go-ahead. After reading the briefs, I felt that the students had overlooked some cases and that two additional issues needed to be addressed. I asked her if I could do some additional research and writing. The rest of the conversation went like this:

Boston Lawyer: "David, I really can't spend much money on this brief. I thought the students' research and arguments were pretty good."

David: "I think I can add to them considerably."

Boston Lawyer: "I can't afford it."

David: "I'll tell you what. I am going to do the research anyway and present you with my additional issues and arguments. If you think my additional work was *really* helpful, you can pay me whatever you want for it. If not, then all you owe me is $350. I feel honored to work for such a prominent lawyer as yourself, and I want to do the best job possible, regardless of how much you pay me."

Boston Lawyer: "All right—if you're willing to assume the risk that I won't be satisfied, go ahead."

I spent another twenty hours on the project, basically rewriting the whole brief. She felt that I had greatly added to the students' work. She asked me how much she owed me. I knew she would not want to pay me another $700 ($35 × 20) on top of the $350 she already owed me, so I suggested that a fair figure would be another $400. She happily agreed.

The point is, to impress a retail lawyer, sometimes you have to guarantee satisfaction (but don't guarantee *results;* the court system is too unpredictable for any lawyer, wholesale or retail, to guarantee results).[1] A guarantee means you are assuming the risk that the retail lawyer will not be satisfied. But you can minimize that risk by working hard and doing whatever you can to please the lawyer. If you can demonstrate your worth to her, she will someday reward you for it, either by paying you a little more on that case, or calling you on another case, or offering you a percentage of her fee in a case.

One advantage of wholesale law practice over retail law practice is that retail lawyers fully understand what wholesale lawyers do, and retail lawyers are willing (except when paying the wholesale lawyer a contingent fee) to pay for good wholesale legal work even if the case does not turn out as successfully as the retail lawyer was hoping; while retail clients, i.e., the nonlawyers whom retail lawyers represent, do not always understand or appreciate what lawyers do, even when they get good results.

Do not offer "satisfaction guaranteed" in every case. Experiment with it, especially with retail lawyers who are on the fence about hiring you. Although retail lawyers understand what wholesale lawyers do, many of them have never actually used a wholesale lawyer before and still need to be convinced. A guarantee of satisfaction is *very* convincing.

Help organize a legal writers section (or wholesale lawyer referral service) within your state and local bar associations

Encourage your state and local bar associations to start legal writers sections or wholesale lawyer referral services so that wholesale legal services can be marketed *en masse* to the retail bar. Offer to be chair or at least a board member. This will establish you as a leader in the movement to integrate wholesale legal services into the everyday practice of law.

Once the legal writers sections or wholesale lawyer referral services are in place and many lawyers who wish to offer wholesale legal services have joined, ask the bar associations to compile a directory of the section/service members and to distribute the directory to retail lawyers. These directories would constitute clearinghouses where retail lawyers could quickly and easily ascertain who and where the wholesale lawyers are, their specialties and qualifications, and perhaps, if a wholesale lawyer wishes to list them, the names of references used, such as those in *Martindale-Hubbell.*

These directories would be a financial boon to the wholesale lawyers and bar associations, as well as a great asset to the retail bar. Because such directories would be costly to produce yet would generate much income for the wholesale lawyers listed, the wholesale lawyers who join and are listed should be willing to pay more than the usual $25 or $40 they pay annually to be members of the other practice sections. They might be willing to pay $100 or more annually. The bar associations could use that money to compile and distribute the directories. It is also conceivable that retail lawyers might be willing to pay something to receive the directories. After all, the ultimate purpose of these sections, services, and directories is to serve the needs of the retail bar and their clients.

In addition to their marketing function, these sections, services, and directories would also enhance the stature of wholesale lawyers within the legal profession.

Note

1. However, some law firms are experimenting with "service guarantees." Robert J. Scott & Jennifer London, "Is Service Guarantee a Client's Joy or Just a Ploy?" *Nat'l L.J.*, Oct. 9, 1995, at D2.

CHAPTER 7

Filling a Gap in the Delivery of Legal Services

Here is a suggestion to mull over.

Despite the huge and growing number of lawyers in this country, millions of low-income Americans still cannot afford a lawyer.[1] Economic logic would seem to dictate that the huge supply of lawyers would drive legal fees down low enough so that all but the truly penniless could afford them. But as Oliver Wendell Holmes said, "The life of the law has not been *logic:* it has been experience."[2] Experience has shown that office overhead costs make it virtually impossible for retail lawyers to lower their fees to the $45 an hour or so which the working poor might be able to pay. A poor person's divorce can be just as complicated and time consuming to handle as a wealthy person's, but most retail lawyers simply cannot devote many hours to matters which pay only $45 an hour. This was explained in a February 26, 1996, *National Law Journal* article[3] by legal ethics professor Geoffrey Hazard about the breakup of Jacoby & Meyers.

Where, then, might we find some lawyers to help the working poor, at least in minor civil matters? Having read this book, you probably think that the last lawyers I have in mind to offer legal services directly to low-income people are wholesale lawyers. After all, wholesale lawyers prefer to limit their client contact. Many wholesale lawyers do not even want to represent people who can afford to pay standard legal fees. Why would they want to represent people who cannot?

The answer is this: creating a wholesale sector of lawyers

would create a large pool of specialized legal talent with low overhead and a willingness to work for low hourly fees. Granted, wholesale lawyers for the most part are not fighters. They might not want to provide complete representation.[4] But they might be willing to counsel some low-income clients, and perhaps even write a letter or make a phone call on behalf of these clients, for, say, $45 per hour, which is slightly more than these wholesale lawyers charge retail lawyers. Admittedly, these low-income people would, in some instances, be represented more effectively and aggressively if they had high-powered retail lawyers. But the point is moot because high-powered retail lawyers do not ordinarily work for $45 an hour. So whatever counseling the wholesale lawyers provide for $45 per hour is better than nothing. It is also better than the alternative that has been suggested in some states: licensing paralegals to do some types of legal work.[5] It is also, arguably, more palatable to the bar than mandatory pro bono.

How can wholesale lawyers help deliver legal services to low-income Americans? Simple. Legal aid organizations and bar-affiliated lawyer referral services could make arrangements with the legal writers sections and wholesale lawyer referral services of bar associations to refer low-income people to section members who volunteer to counsel a certain number of these people per year for $45 an hour (or less, if the wholesale lawyer is willing to accept less). Participation by the wholesale lawyers would be strictly voluntary.

No wholesale lawyer would be referred a client whom a retail lawyer is willing to represent. Wholesale lawyers should not be competing with retail lawyers in this arena, for the wholesale lawyers have an unfair advantage: low overhead. So if a wholesale lawyer were to accept a referral, the wholesale lawyer would not be permitted to earn more than $45 an hour in that particular matter or in any future matter that client might have. If at some point the client has a substantial fee-generating case, the wholesale lawyer would either have to refer the case back to the lawyer referral service for referral to a retail lawyer who is not on the wholesale referral list or would have to charge a low ($45 an hour or less) hourly rate with no contingent fee.

This is by no means a complete solution to the problem of delivering legal services to low-income people, but it might help.

Notes

1. *See generally* Karen E. Kelleher, "The Availability Crisis in Legal Services: A Turning Point for the Profession," 6 *Geo. J. Legal Ethics* 953 (1993) ("If we have so many lawyers, why are so many people going unrepresented?").

2. Oliver Wendell Holmes, Jr., *The Common Law* 1 (1881) (emphasis added).

3. Geoffrey C. Hazard, "Firm's Muddy Mission," *Nat'l L.J.*, Feb. 26, 1996, at A21.

4. *See* Amy Stevens, "Do-It-Yourselfers Take On Some Services to Keep Costs Down," *Wall Street Journal,* Nov. 6, 1995, at B10 (Los Angeles lawyer Forrest "Woody" Mosten and other lawyers provide limited service to modest-income clients while encouraging these clients to undertake certain aspects of the representation themselves. Mosten calls this "unbundling."); ABA Comm'n on Nonlawyer Practice, *Nonlawyer Activity in Law-Related Situations* 121 (1995) (Rules and Policy Relating to Limited Forms of Assistance By Lawyers).

5. Roger C. Cramton, "Delivery of Legal Services to Ordinary Americans," 44 *Case Wes. Res. L. Rev.* 531, 573–74 (1994); *see also* Deborah L. Rhode, "The Delivery of Legal Services by Non-Lawyers," 4 *Geo. J. Legal Ethics* 209 (1990).

CONCLUSION

When Every Lawyer Is Your Friend

When you are a wholesale lawyer, every lawyer is your friend. Every lawyer is a potential customer. Every lawyer is someone you can help. Every lawyer you deal with on a direct basis is on *your* side, not against you. You rarely have hostile relations with other lawyers. In fact, you rarely have hostile relations with anyone.

Wholesale law practice stimulates your mind without wracking your nerves. You spend your day the way law professors and appellate judges do: thinking about the law, writing about the law, and discussing the law with colleagues who you are trying to educate, persuade, and help, rather than beat. But unlike law professors and appellate judges, who are somewhat isolated from the excitement and social interaction of everyday law practice, you are in the thick of it. You help practicing lawyers handle cases and transactions; you lunch with practicing lawyers; you talk to practicing lawyers in the courthouse, on the street, and in their offices; you play golf and go to the theatre with practicing lawyers. Your role in the everyday practice of law is, admittedly, not a starring one. It is a supporting role. But it is an important, enjoyable, and peaceful role; and it might be just the role for you.

APPENDIX A

ABA Committee on Ethics and Professional Responsibility Formal Opinion 88-356

Formal Opinion 88-356—December 16, 1988

Temporary Lawyers

In order to satisfy the requirements of the Model Rules and predecessor Model Code when a lawyer is engaged temporarily to work for clients of a law firm (including a corporate legal department), the lawyer and the firm must exercise care, in accordance with the guidelines in this opinion, to avoid conflicts of interest, to maintain confidentiality of information relating to the representation of clients, to disclose to clients the arrangement between the lawyer and the firm in some circumstances, and to comply with other applicable provisions of the Rules and Code. The use of a lawyer placement agency to obtain temporary lawyer services where the agency's fee is a proportion of the lawyer's compensation does not violate the Model Rules or predecessor Model Code as long as the professional independence of the lawyer is maintained without interference by the agency, the total fee paid by each client to the law firm is reasonable, and the arrangement otherwise is in accord with the guidelines in this opinion.

The Committee has received a number of inquiries relating to the increasing use by law firms of temporary lawyers.[1] The temporary lawyer may work on a single matter for the firm or may work generally for the firm for a limited period, typically to meet temporary staffing needs of the firm or to provide special expertise not available in the firm and needed for work on a specific matter. The temporary lawyer may work in the firm's office or may visit the office only occasionally when the work requires. The temporary lawyer may work exclusively for the firm during a period of temporary employment or may work simultaneously on other matters for other firms.

In this opinion, the Committee addresses ethical issues affecting the firm and the temporary lawyer involving the application to temporary lawyer practice of rules relating to conflicts of interest; confidentiality of client information; disclosure to the client of arrangements between the firm and the lawyer (including fee division); and arrangements with lawyer placement agencies. These issues are addressed under the Model Rules and the predecessor Model Code.

Conflicts of Interest

In the Model Rules, the general conflict of interest provision is Rule 1.7, which standing alone applies only to an individual lawyer and a client about to be represented or currently represented by that lawyer. Rule 1.7 prohibits a lawyer from representing a client if the representation of that client will be directly adverse to another client or may be materially limited by the lawyer's responsibilities to another client or to a third person or by the lawyer's own interests, unless the lawyer reasonably believes that there will be no adverse effect (as described in the Rule), and the client consents after consultation.

Rule 1.9 relates to conflicts of interest involving former clients of a lawyer. It provides:

> A lawyer who has formerly represented a client in a matter shall not thereafter: (a) represent another person in the same or a substantially related matter in which that person's interests are materially adverse to the interests of the former client unless the former client consents after consultation; or (b) use information relating to the representation to the disadvantage of the client except as Rule 1.6 or Rule 3.3 would permit or require with respect to a client or when the information has become generally known.

It is clear that a temporary lawyer who works on a matter for a client of a firm with whom the temporary lawyer is temporarily associated "represents" that client for purposes of Rules 1.7 and 1.9. Thus, a temporary lawyer could not, under Rule 1.7, work simultaneously on matters for clients of different firms if the representation of each were directly adverse to the other (in the absence of client consent and subject to the other conditions set forth in the Rule). Similarly, under Rule 1.9, a temporary lawyer who worked on a matter for a client of one firm could not thereafter work for a client of another firm on the same or a substantially related matter in which that client's interests are materially adverse to the interests of the client of the first firm (in the absence of consent of the former client and subject to the other conditions stated in the Rule).[2]

DR 5-105(A) and DR 5-105(B) of the Model Code require a lawyer to decline employment if it will or is likely adversely to affect the lawyer's independent judgment in behalf of an existing client or would involve the representation of differing interests, except with the informed consent of both clients and then only where it is obvious that the lawyer can represent adequately the interests of each. DR 5-105(C). Thus, a temporary lawyer could not, under DR 5-105, work simultaneously for clients of different firms with differing interests except as permitted by DR 5-105(C).[3]

The most difficult conflict of interest questions involving temporary lawyers arise under the imputed disqualification provisions of Rule 1.10, which provides:

> (a) While lawyers are associated in a firm, none of them shall knowingly represent a client when any one of them practicing alone would be prohibited from doing so by Rules 1.7, 1.8(c), 1.9 or 2.2.
>
> (b) When a lawyer becomes associated with a firm, the firm may not knowingly represent a person in the same or a substantially related matter in which that lawyer, or a firm with which the lawyer was associated, had previously represented a client whose interests are materially adverse to that person and about whom the lawyer had acquired information protected by Rules 1.6 and 1.9(b) that is material to the matter.
>
> (c) When a lawyer has terminated an association with a firm, the firm is not prohibited from thereafter representing a person with interests materially adverse to those of a client represented by the formerly associated lawyer unless:

> (1) the matter is the same or substantially related to that in which the formerly associated lawyer represented the client; and
>
> (2) any lawyer remaining in the firm has information protected by Rules 1.6 and 1.9(b) that is material to the matter.
>
> (d) A disqualification prescribed by this rule may be waived by the affected client under the conditions stated in Rule 1.7.[4]

The basic question is under what circumstances a temporary lawyer should be treated as "associated in a firm" or "associated with a firm."[5] The question whether a temporary lawyer is associated with a firm at any time must be determined by a functional analysis of the facts and circumstances involved in the relationship between the temporary lawyer and the firm consistent with the purposes for the Rule. The Comment to Rule 1.10, although not addressing specifically the temporary lawyer situation, provides helpful guidance. It provides in relevant part:

> For purposes of the Rules of Professional Conduct, the term "firm" includes lawyers in a private firm, and lawyers employed in the legal department of a corporation or other organization, or in a legal services organization. Whether two or more lawyers constitute a firm within this definition can depend on the specific facts. For example, two practitioners who share office space and occasionally consult or assist each other ordinarily would not be regarded as constituting a firm. However, if they present themselves to the public in a way suggesting that they are a firm or conduct themselves as a firm, they should be regarded as a firm for purposes of the Rules. The terms of any formal agreement between associated lawyers are relevant in determining whether they are a firm, as is the fact that they have mutual access to confidential information concerning the clients they serve. Furthermore, it is relevant in doubtful cases to consider the underlying purpose of the rule that is involved. A group of lawyers could be regarded as a firm for purposes of the rule that the same lawyer should not represent opposing parties in litigation, while it might not be so regarded for purposes of the rule that information acquired by one lawyer is attributed to another.
>
> * * *
>
> When lawyers have been associated in a firm but then end their association, however, the problem is more complicated. The fiction that the law firm is the same as a single lawyer is no longer wholly realistic. There are several competing considerations. First, the client previously represented must be reasonably assured that the principle

> of loyalty to the client is not compromised. Second, the rule of disqualification should not be so broadly cast as to preclude other persons from having reasonable choice of legal counsel. Third, the rule of disqualification should not unreasonably hamper lawyers from forming new associations and taking on new clients after having left a previous association. In this connection, it should be recognized that today many lawyers practice in firms, that many to some degree limit their practice to one field or another, and that many move from one association to another several times in their careers. If the concept of imputed disqualification were defined with unqualified rigor, the result would be radical curtailment of the opportunity of lawyers to move from one practice setting to another and of the opportunity of clients to change counsel.

After discussion of the two traditional rubrics under which these competing principles have in the past been explained, the Comment notes that a rule based on functional analysis is more appropriate for determining imputed disqualification. Noting that two functions are involved, preserving confidentiality and avoiding positions adverse to a client, the Comment continues:

> Preserving confidentiality is a question of access to information. Access to information, in turn, is essentially a question of fact in particular circumstances, aided by inferences, deductions or working presumptions that reasonably may be made about the way in which lawyers work together. A lawyer may have general access to files of all clients of a law firm and may regularly participate in discussions of their affairs; it should be inferred that such a lawyer in fact is privy to all information about all the firm's clients. In contrast, another lawyer may have access to the files of only a limited number of clients and participate in discussion of the affairs of no other clients; in the absence of information to the contrary, it should be inferred that such a lawyer in fact is privy to information about the clients actually served but not those of other clients.
>
> Application of paragraphs (b) and (c) [of Rule 1.10] depends on a situation's particular facts. In any such inquiry, the burden of proof should rest upon the firm whose disqualification is sought.
>
> Paragraphs (b) and (c) operate to disqualify the firm only when the lawyer involved has actual knowledge of information protected by Rules 1.6 and 1.9(b). Thus, if a lawyer while with one firm acquired no knowledge of information relating to a particular client of the firm, and that lawyer later joined another firm, neither the lawyer individually nor the second firm is disqualified from representing

> another client in the same or a related matter even though the interests of the two clients conflict.
>
> * * *
>
> The second aspect of loyalty to client is the lawyer's obligation to decline subsequent representations involving positions adverse to a former client arising in substantially related matters. This obligation requires abstention from adverse representation by the individual lawyer involved, but does not properly entail abstention of other lawyers through imputed disqualification. Hence, this aspect of the problem is governed by Rule 1.9(a). Thus, if a lawyer left one firm for another, the new affiliation would not preclude the firms involved from continuing to represent clients with adverse interests in the same or related matters so long as the conditions of paragraphs (b) and (c) concerning confidentiality have been met.

Ultimately, whether a temporary lawyer is treated as being "associated with a firm" while working on a matter for the firm depends on whether the nature of the relationship is such that the temporary lawyer has access to information relating to the representation of firm clients other than the client on whose matters the lawyer is working and the consequent risk of improper disclosure or misuse of information relating to representation of other clients of the firm. For example, a temporary lawyer who works for a firm, in the firm office, on a number of matters for different clients, under circumstances where the temporary lawyer is likely to have access to information relating to the representation of other firm clients, may well be deemed to be "associated with" the firm generally under Rule 1.10 as to all other clients of the firm, unless the firm, through accurate records or otherwise, can demonstrate that the temporary lawyer had access to information relating to the representation only of certain other clients. If such limited access can be demonstrated, then the temporary lawyer should not be deemed to be "associated with" the firm under Rule 1.10. Also, if a temporary lawyer works with a firm only on a single matter under circumstances like the collaboration of two independent firms on a single case, where the temporary lawyer has no access to information relating to the representation of other firm clients, the temporary lawyer should not be deemed "associated with" the firm generally for purposes of application of Rule 1.10. This is particularly true where the temporary lawyer has no ongoing relationship with the firm and does not regularly work in the firm's office under circumstances likely to result in disclosure of information relating to the representation of other firm clients.

As the direct connection between the temporary lawyer and the work on matters involving conflicts of interest between clients of two firms becomes more remote, it becomes more appropriate not to apply Rule 1.10 to disqualify a firm from representation of its clients or to prohibit the employment of the temporary lawyer. Whether Rule 1.10 requires imputed disqualification must be determined case by case on the basis of all relevant facts and circumstances, unless disqualification is clear under the Rules.

The distinction drawn between when a temporary lawyer is or is not associated with a firm is only a guideline to the ultimate determination and not a set rule. For example, if a temporary lawyer was directly involved in work on a matter for a client of a firm and had knowledge of material information relating to the representation of that client, it would be inadvisable for a second firm representing other parties in the same matter whose interests are directly adverse to those of the client of the first firm to engage the temporary lawyer during the pendency of the matter, even for work on other matters. The second firm should make appropriate inquiry and should not hire the temporary lawyer or use the temporary lawyer on a matter if doing so would disqualify the firm from continuing its representation of a client on a pending matter.

Although at the time of the adoption of the Model Code in 1969 the temporary lawyer phenomenon had not yet appeared, the purpose of DR 5-105(D),[6] the imputed disqualification provision of the Code, coincides with the purpose of Rule 1.10. The Committee is of the opinion that the foregoing functional analysis applies equally under DR 5-105(D).

For the reasons discussed above, in order to minimize the risk of disqualification, firms should, to the extent practicable, screen each temporary lawyer from all information relating to clients for which the temporary lawyer does no work. All law firms employing temporary lawyers also should maintain a complete and accurate record of all matters on which each temporary lawyer works. A temporary lawyer working with several firms should make every effort to avoid exposure within those firms to any information relating to clients on whose matters the temporary lawyer is not working. Since a temporary lawyer has a coequal interest in avoiding future imputed disqualification, the temporary lawyer should also maintain a record of clients and matters worked on.

Confidentiality of Information

Model Rule 1.6 prohibits revealing "information relating to representation of a client," subject to exceptions set forth in the Rule. The Rule applies to each lawyer in a firm with respect to each client of the firm and not solely to clients with whom that lawyer works. The prohibition against revealing information relating to representation of a client serves its purpose only to the extent that each lawyer with a firm (who may have information about any firm client) is bound by the Rule with respect to each client of the firm. Similarly, the temporary lawyer who works for a firm on matters of a firm client is bound by Rule 1.6 not to reveal information relating to the representation of that client (except as otherwise authorized by the Rule). The temporary lawyer also is bound not to reveal information relating to representation of other clients of the firm which the temporary lawyer learns as a result of working with the firm.

The application of Rule 1.6 does not, however, generally depend upon the source of information relating to representation of a client. Thus, a lawyer with a firm is prohibited from revealing information relating to representation of a client of the firm even if the lawyer's knowledge of the information did not arise from the representation or through the firm and even if knowledge was acquired before the lawyer-client relationship existed.

In contrast, the definition of protected information set forth in DR 4-101 of the Code is narrower than that of Rule 1.6. DR 4-101 protects information subject to the attorney-client privilege and information "gained in the professional relationship" which would be embarrassing or detrimental to the client or which the client has asked be held inviolate.[7]

The extent to which the prohibitions in the Rules against revealing protected information will affect a temporary lawyer depends on the nature of the relationship between the temporary lawyer and the firm. Thus, a temporary lawyer who works for a firm, in the firm office, on a number of matters for different clients, under circumstances where the temporary lawyer is likely to have access to information relating to the representation of other firm clients ordinarily would be deemed to be "associated with" the firm as to all other clients of the firm, unless through accurate records or otherwise, it can be demonstrated that the temporary lawyer had access to information relating to the representation only of certain other clients. If such limited access cannot be demonstrated, the temporary lawyer in that situation must not disclose information relating to the representation of persons known to the lawyer to be firm clients regardless of the source of the information.

Under other circumstances, however, the relationship of the firm with the temporary lawyer is more like the relationship between a firm and a totally independent lawyer. This ordinarily is the case where the temporary lawyer has been screened from access to information relating to the representation of firm clients for whom the temporary lawyer is not working, whether the temporary lawyer is working in the firm office or not. In that situation, the temporary lawyer's obligations under Rule 1.6 are, in the Committee's opinion, limited to not revealing (1) information relating to the representation of any client for whom the temporary lawyer is working, and (2) information relating to the representation of other firm clients only to the extent that the temporary lawyer in fact obtains the information as a result of working with the firm.

Thus, where the temporary lawyer is in a position to have obtained information relating to the representation of other clients in the course of employment by the firm, it is assumed for purposes of the Rules that such information was in fact learned in that capacity. On the other hand, where the temporary lawyer actually has information relating to the representation of a firm client which could not have been obtained in the course of employment by the firm, the Rule is no more applicable to the temporary lawyer than it would be to a totally independent lawyer associated with a firm in a particular matter only, who obtains information relating to the representation of firm clients other than through working with the firm.

The same standards apply with respect to other provisions of the Rules which relate to disclosure or use of information relating to representation of a client, such as Rule 1.8(b) prohibiting use of such information to the disadvantage of the client.[8]

Under the Code, the temporary lawyer could learn "confidences" and "secrets" of firm clients, as defined in DR 4-101, only as a direct result of working with the firm. When the relationship with the firm is limited, it is less likely that the temporary lawyer will learn confidences or secrets about firm clients for whom the temporary lawyer is not working. However, under the Code, if the temporary lawyer does learn the confidences or secrets of a firm client, then the temporary lawyer must not reveal those confidences or secrets regardless of the nature of the temporary lawyer's relationship with the firm.

Supervising lawyers with the firm also have an obligation to make reasonable efforts to ensure that the temporary lawyer conforms to the rules of professional conduct, including those governing the confidentiality of information relating to representation of a client. Rule 5.1(b) and (c); DR 4-101(D).[9]

Disclosure to Client

Rule 7.5(d), which prohibits lawyers from implying that they practice in a partnership or other organization when that is not the fact, articulates the underlying policy that a client is entitled to know who or what entity is representing the client. A question therefore arises as to whether the client must be told that a temporary lawyer engaged by the firm is working on the client's matter as well as other information relating to the arrangement between the firm and the temporary lawyer. Relevant to the inquiry are Rule 1.2(a), requiring a lawyer to consult with the client as to the means by which the client's objectives are to be pursued, and Rule 1.4, relating to client communication.

The Committee is of the opinion that where the temporary lawyer is performing independent work for a client without the close supervision of a lawyer associated with the law firm, the client must be advised of the fact that the temporary lawyer will work on the client's matter and the consent of the client must be obtained. This is so because the client, by retaining the firm, cannot reasonably be deemed to have consented to the involvement of an independent lawyer. On the other hand, where the temporary lawyer is working under the direct supervision of a lawyer associated with the firm, the fact that a temporary lawyer will work on the client's matter will not ordinarily have to be disclosed to the client. A client who retains a firm expects that the legal services will be rendered by lawyers and other personnel closely supervised by the firm. Client consent to the involvement of firm personnel and the disclosure to those personnel of confidential information necessary to the representation is inherent in the act of retaining the firm.[10]

Assuming that a law firm simply pays the temporary lawyer reasonable compensation for the services performed for the firm and does not charge the payments thereafter to the client as a disbursement, the firm has no obligation to reveal to the client the compensation arrangement with the temporary lawyer. Rule 1.5(e), relating to division of a fee between lawyers, does not apply in this instance because the gross fee the client pays the firm is not shared with the temporary lawyer. The payments to the temporary lawyer are like compensation paid to nonlawyer employees for services and could also include a percentage of firm net profits without violation of the Rules or the predecessor Code. *See* ABA Informal Opinion 1440 (1979).

If, however, the arrangement between the firm and the temporary lawyer involves a direct division of the actual fee paid by the client, such as percentage division of a contingent fee, then Rule 1.5(e)(1) requires the consent of the client and satisfaction of the other requirements of the Rule regardless of the extent of the supervision.

The requirement of Rule 1.5(a) that the total fee be reasonable is, of course, a restriction only on the fee charged to the client and not on how much is paid to the temporary lawyer. That requirement must be satisfied in all events.

EC 7-7 and EC 7-8 are Code analogues to Rules 1.2(a) and 1.4 defining the obligations of the law firm in informing a client of the use of a temporary lawyer and, in appropriate instances, to obtain client consent. The Committee notes that DR 2-107(A) of the Code requires client consent to a division of fees between lawyers and that EC 2-22 provides: "Without the consent of his client, a lawyer should not associate in a particular matter another lawyer outside his firm." The Committee nevertheless is of the opinion that where a temporary lawyer is working under the close firm supervision described above, such employment does not involve "association with a lawyer outside the firm," within the meaning of this Ethical Consideration. The underlying purposes of the Rule and Code provisions and their functional analyses are similar. For the reasons set forth above, absent a division with the temporary lawyer of the actual fee paid by the client to the firm, the client need not be informed of the financial arrangement with the temporary lawyer under the Model Code since it does not involve a division of the gross fee between lawyers.

Arrangements With Placement Agencies

Law firms wishing to hire temporary lawyers frequently use lawyer placement or other employment agencies. Questions have been raised whether a law firm which engages a temporary lawyer through such an agency may pay the agency a fee which is a percentage of the compensation paid by the law firm to the temporary lawyer without violating the provisions of Model Rule 5.4 or DR 3-102(a) of the Code.[11]

Arrangements among placement agencies, law firms and temporary lawyers vary. Usually the law firm will contact the placement agency and provide general information as to the nature of the matter and the area of practice and level of experience desired in the temporary lawyer.

The placement agency maintains files on attorneys willing to accept independent contractor assignments or may recruit a lawyer with the desired capabilities and will attempt to match the lawyer with the task and attributes needed by the law firm. Some agencies allow each attorney to establish his or her own hourly rate, and this will be part of the information in the file of that attorney maintained by the placement agency. The placement agency informs the law firm of the name and background of the lawyer and the hourly cost to the law firm for that lawyer's services. This hourly cost includes the attorney's hourly rate as set by the lawyer and the fee to be paid to the placement agency, which is either a fixed hourly sum that does not vary in relation to the temporary lawyer's hourly rate or a percentage of the lawyer's compensation. Under either arrangement, the amount of the placement agency's fee will, of course, vary with the number of hours worked by the temporary lawyer for the law firm on the engagement.

This Committee is of the opinion that an arrangement whereby a law firm pays to a temporary lawyer compensation in a fixed dollar amount or at an hourly rate and pays a placement agency a fee based upon a percentage of the lawyer's compensation, does not involve the sharing of legal fees by a lawyer with a nonlawyer in violation of Rule 5.4 or DR 3-102(A) of the Code. There is a distinction between the character of the compensation paid to the lawyer and the compensation paid to the placement agency. The temporary lawyer is paid by the law firm for the services the lawyer performs under supervision of the firm for a client of the firm. The placement agency is compensated for locating, recruiting, screening and providing the temporary lawyer for the law firm just as agencies are compensated for placing with law firms nonlawyer personnel (whether temporary or permanent).

Moreover, even assuming there is a total amount comprised of a lawyer's compensation and the placement agency fee that is split, the total is not a "legal fee" under the commonly understood meaning of the term. A legal fee is paid by a client to a lawyer. Here the law firm bills the client and is paid a legal fee for services to the client. The fee paid by the client to the firm ordinarily would include the total paid the lawyer and the agency, and also may include charges for overhead and profit. There is no direct payment of a "legal fee" by the client to the temporary lawyer or by the client to the placement agency out of which either pays the other.

In addition, the rationale for the rule forbidding the sharing of legal fees with nonlawyers, the maintenance of the lawyer's professional independence, does not support the view that these arrangements involve fee-splitting. The title of Rule 5.4 itself focuses on this underlying rationale: "Professional Independence of a Lawyer." In Formal Opinion 87-355 (December 5, 1987), the Committee concluded that the sponsor of a for-profit prepaid legal service plan might retain a portion of the monthly fee paid by plan members to cover the plan sponsor's overhead and profit without violating the fee-sharing prohibitions of Rule 5.4 or of Rule 7.2(c) (prohibition against giving anything of value to a person for recommending a lawyer's services). That opinion restated the two principal reasons for the fee-sharing prohibition: "first, to avoid the possibility of a nonlawyer being able to interfere with the exercise of a lawyer's independent professional judgment in representing a client; and second, to insure that the total fee paid by a client is not unreasonably high." *See also* Informal Opinion 1440 (1979) (a law firm's compensation arrangement with its office administrator, including payment of a percentage of the net profits of the law firm, did not involve improper fee-splitting).

The Committee perceives no adverse impact upon the exercise of the temporary lawyer's independent professional judgment in the lawyer's work for the law firm which results from payment of a placement agency fee as a percentage of or in proportion to the lawyer's compensation. The same factors that are present in any law firm which relates its compensation of lawyers to the time worked by the lawyer are presented by the arrangement here. The only variation is that another payment in relation to the time spent by the lawyer is paid for a different service to a third party, the placement agency.

With respect to the reasonableness of the total fee to each client on whose matters the temporary lawyer works, the case is no different than that of a law firm hiring a temporary secretary or other temporary help through an agency. There is no meaningful difference between the practice of lawyer placement agencies charging a fee to a law firm for recruiting a permanent associate or partner, which often is a percentage of the lawyer's first year compensation (a practice not challenged), and a fee based on the temporary lawyer's actual compensation paid over a period of less than a year. There is no reason to assume that the actual cost to the law firm of the temporary lawyer hired through an agency (and consequently the impact on the fee to the client) would be higher than the cost of that lawyer's services hired direct by the firm, without the intervention of a placement agency. The increasing use of placement agencies for temporary lawyers lends support to the view that this is an efficient and cost-effective way for law firms to manage their work flow and deployment of resources.

The Committee is aware that the temporary lawyer often is on a permanent roster maintained by the placement agency and may wish repeated placements by the agency with a succession of law firms. This factor conceivably could limit the temporary lawyer's exercise of independent professional judgment in some respects because of the lawyer's need to maintain the goodwill of the placement agency. *See* ABA Formal Opinion 87-355, Section I, and ABA Formal Opinion 87-354. Unlike the situation in those opinions where the lawyers are dealing directly with clients, here the temporary lawyer is working for a law firm which itself has supervisory obligations over the temporary lawyer by the provisions of Rule 5.1. But as long as the temporary lawyer avoids the excessive controls exercised by nonlawyers noted in those opinions, the arrangement is in our opinion permissible under the constraints imposed by the Rules and the predecessor Code.[12]

Sound practice suggests that the agreement between a temporary lawyer and a placement agency should make clear in explicit terms that the agency will not exercise any control or influence over the exercise of professional judgment by the lawyer, including limiting or extending the amount of time the lawyer spends on work for the clients of the employing firm. Moreover, the law firm must make certain that the compensation received by the temporary lawyer, whether paid directly by the firm to the lawyer or paid by the placement agency to the lawyer from sums which the firm pays the agency, is adequate to satisfy the firm that it may expect the work to be performed competently for the firm's clients. These matters fall within the responsibilities of the law firm.

In summary, both the temporary lawyer and the law firm hiring the lawyer must be sensitive to the need to protect and prevent misuse of information relating to the representation (or under the Code, the secrets or confidences) of firm clients. The application of the conflicts rules of the Model Rules or the predecessor Model Code depend upon all the facts and circumstances of the arrangement between the temporary lawyer and the firm in accordance with the general guidelines discussed in this opinion. Disclosure to a firm client on whose matters the temporary lawyer works of the arrangement with a temporary lawyer may be required, except where the temporary lawyer is working under the direct supervision of a lawyer associated with the firm. Provided the temporary lawyer maintains independence of professional judgment against any influence by a placement agency, the law firm may pay placement agency fees, even where the amount of the fees is related to the amount of the temporary lawyer's compensation.

Notes

1. For purposes of this opinion, "firm" or "law firm" includes a sole practitioner and a corporate legal department. *See* ABA Model Rules of Professional Conduct (1983, amended 1987), Terminology, Rule 1.10 Comment. The term "temporary lawyer" means a lawyer engaged by a firm for a limited period, either directly or through a lawyer placement agency. The term does not, however, include a lawyer who works part time for a firm or full time but without contemplation of permanent employment, who is nevertheless engaged by the firm as an employee for an extended period and does legal work only for that firm. That person's relationship with the firm, during the period of employment, is more like the relationship of an associate of the firm, and the Model Rules or the predecessor Model Code of Professional Responsibility (1969, amended 1980) will govern the lawyer and the firm and their relationship as with any associate of the firm. Similarly, "temporary lawyer" does not include a lawyer who has an "of counsel" relationship with a law firm or who is retained in a matter as independent associated counsel.

2. The consent of the current client may also be required under Rule 1.7(b).

3. The Code does not address specifically representation of a client with interests adverse to a former client, but the standards relating to confidentiality and disqualification rules applied by the courts ordinarily would prohibit representation of the second client under the Code in the same circumstances as under the Rules.

4. The Comment to Rule 1.10 explains the Rule as follows: "The rule of imputed disqualification stated in paragraph (a) gives effect to the principle of loyalty to the client as it applies to lawyers who practice in a law firm. Such situations can be considered from the premise that a firm of lawyers is essentially one lawyer for purposes of the rules governing loyalty to the client, or from the premise that each lawyer is vicariously bound by the obligation of loyalty owed by each lawyer with whom the lawyer is associated. Paragraph (a) operates only among the lawyers currently associated in a firm. When a lawyer moves from one firm to another, the situation is governed by paragraphs (b) and (c)."

5. Based on a reading of the entire Rule and the Comment to the Rule and an analysis of the reasons for the restrictions in the Rule, the Committee perceives no substantive difference between the terms "in" and "with" in the context of the Rule.

6. DR 5-105(D) provides: "If a lawyer is required to decline employment or to withdraw from employment under a Disciplinary Rule, no partner, or associate, or any other lawyer affiliated with him or his firm, may accept or continue such employment." *See also* Footnote 4, *supra.*

7. DR 4-101(A) provides: " 'Confidence' refers to information protected by the attorney-client privilege under applicable law, and 'secret' refers to other information gained in the professional relationship that the client has requested be held inviolate or the disclosure of which would be embarrassing or would be likely to be detrimental to the client."

8. *See* Rule 1.9(b) and the Comment to Rule 1.10 quoted *supra.* The Code

analogue, DR 4-101(D), applies only with respect to disclosures of client confidences and secrets.

9. Rule 5.1(b) provides: "A lawyer having direct supervisory authority over another lawyer shall make reasonable efforts to ensure that the other lawyer conforms to the Rules of Professional Conduct." Rule 5.1(c) provides: "A lawyer shall be responsible for another lawyer's violation of the Rules of Professional Conduct if: (1) the lawyer orders or, with knowledge of the specific conduct, ratifies the conduct involved; or (2) the lawyer is a partner in the law firm in which the other lawyer practices, or has direct supervisory authority over the other lawyer, and knows of the conduct at a time when its consequences can be avoided or mitigated but fails to take reasonable remedial action." The temporary lawyer, of course, also remains subject to the Rules. Rule 5.2(a) thus provides: "A lawyer is bound by the Rules of Professional Conduct notwithstanding that the lawyer acted at the direction of another person." The only analogue in the Code to Rules 5.1 and 5.2 is DR 1-103(A) which requires disclosure to the proper tribunal or authority of a lawyer's unprivileged knowledge of the misconduct of another lawyer. Both the temporary lawyer and the lawyers with the firm engaging the temporary lawyer retain all the general obligations of lawyers prescribed by the Model Rules. For example, the lawyers with the firm have the obligation to provide competent representation to the client under Rule 1.1, as does the temporary lawyer who undertakes work for the client. *See* DR 6-101 of the Code.

10. *See* Rule 1.6 and the Comment to Rule 1.6 which provides in part: "Lawyers in a firm may, in the course of the firm's practice, disclose to each other information relating to the representation of the client of the firm unless the client has instructed that particular information be confined to specified lawyers."

11. The Committee on Professional and Judicial Ethics of the Association of the Bar of the City of New York in Opinion No. 1988-3, April 6, 1988 (amended in Opinion No. 1988-3-A, May 23, 1988), concluded that an arrangement under which the law firm pays the agency and the agency, after retaining a percentage as its fee, pays the lawyer constitutes improper sharing of fees with a nonlawyer and aiding in the unauthorized practice of law by the placement agency in violation of the New York Lawyer's Code of Professional Responsibility. The Committee also found infirm an arrangement where the law firm pays the lawyer directly and pays the agency a placement fee related to the compensation paid to the lawyer. The Committee on Professional Ethics of the Connecticut Bar Association in Informal Opinion 88-15 (August 1, 1988) concluded that an arrangement under which the law firm pays the lawyer's compensation direct to the lawyer and separately pays the placement agency its fee based on a percentage of the lawyer's compensation does not violate the Connecticut Rules of Professional Conduct.

12. One could, of course, hypothesize the operation by nonlawyers of an agency which places lawyers directly with clients (and not through the legal department of the client) who pay compensation to the agency for the lawyers' services. But in such a case the agency would not only be sharing fees with its lawyers but would almost certainly be engaged in unauthorized practice of law under the law of every American jurisdiction.

APPENDIX B

Mixed hourly/contingent fee engagement letter

RETAIL Q. LAWYER
Main Street
U.S.A.

Wholesale Z. Lawyer
State Street
U.S.A.

RE: My Client, John Jones (Client)

Dear WL:

As a followup to our phone conversation, this letter will confirm that you will be working with me on Client's case, and I will pay you $25 per hour until you have expended 20 hours in the case. After you have expended 20 hours, your fee will be contingent upon a recovery in the case: you will receive twenty (20%) percent of my fee in the case, my fee being one-third of what Client recovers. You will do all research and paperwork in the case and be reasonable available for consultation with me and for meeting with Client in my office.

Very truly yours,

RL

Short-form contingent fee agreement

CONTINGENCY FEE AGREEMENT BETWEEN LAWYER AND WHOLESALE LAWYER

WHEREAS, Retail Lawyer (RL) is representing Client in connection with a ________________ case and has a contingent-fee agreement with Client wherein RL will receive one-third (1/3) of the gross recovery collected;

NOW, THEREFORE, RL and Wholesale Lawyer (WL) agree that WL will provide support services to RL in connection with Client's case. WL will do all necessary legal research and will write all pleadings, discovery requests/responses, briefs, and other documents; and will be available on reasonable notice for consultation with RL. In exchange for WL's services, RL agrees to pay WL one-third (1/3) of RL's collected fee from Client's case.

RL will be responsible for communications with Client and with opposing counsel and will be counsel of record in Client's case. WL need not file an appearance in Client's case unless WL wishes and RL consents. However, WL agrees to attend meetings between RL and Client, meetings between RL and opposing counsel, depositions, preliminary court hearings, and trial.

This Agreement is not assignable or delegable by WL.

RL and WL agree that any disputes over this Agreement will be submitted to binding arbitration with each paying his own costs.

______________________________	______________________________
(Retail Lawyer)	(Wholesale Lawyer)

____

(Date)

Selected Books From...

THE SECTION OF LAW PRACTICE MANAGEMENT

ABA Guide to Lawyer Trust Accounts. This book deals with how lawyers should manage trust accounts to comply with ethical & statutory requirements.

ABA Guide to Legal Marketing. A collection of new and innovative marketing ideas and strategies for lawyers and firms.

ABA Guide to Professional Managers in the Law Office. This book provides guidelines that show how professional management can and does work. It shows lawyers how to practice more efficiently by delegating management tasks to professional managers.

Becoming Computer Literate. A guide to computer basics for lawyers and other legal professionals.

Billing Innovations. This book looks at innovative fee arrangements and how your approach toward billing can deeply affect the attorney-client relationship. It also explains how billing and pricing are absolutely intertwined with strategic planning, maintaining quality of services, marketing, instituting a compensation system, and firm governance.

Changing Jobs, 2nd Ed. A handbook designed to help lawyers make changes in their professional careers. Includes career planning advice from nearly 50 experts.

Compensation Plans for Law Firms, 2nd Ed. This second edition discusses the basics for a fair and simple compensation system for partners, of counsel, associates, paralegals, and staff.

Do-It-Yourself Public Relations. A hands-on guide for lawyers with public relations ideas, sample letters and forms. The book includes a diskette that includes model letters to the press that have paid off in news stories and media attention.

Finding the Right Lawyer. This guide answers the questions people should ask when searching for legal counsel. It includes a glossary of legal specialties and the ten questions you should ask a lawyer before hiring.

Flying Solo: A Survival Guide for the Solo Lawyer, 2nd ed. An updated and expanded guide to the problems and issues unique to the solo practitioner.

How to Draft Bills Clients Rush to Pay. A collection of techniques for drafting bills that project honesty, competence, fairness and value and how draft an inviting statement.

How to Get and Keep Good Clients, 2nd ed. Best-selling author and acknowledged marketing ace Jay Foonberg gives time-proven tips and techniques that you can use for long-range and immediate marketing success.

How to Start and Build a Law Practice, 3rd ed. Jay Foonberg's classic guide has been updated and expanded. Included are more than 10 new chapters on marketing, financing, automation, practicing from home, ethics and professional responsibility.

Law Office Staff Manual for Solos and Small Firms. A book to help solo and small firm practitioners set up their own law office staff manuals. It includes a diskette containing the text of the manual. The diskette is in WordPerfect 5.1 and ASCHII formats.

Lawyer's Guide to the Internet. A no-nonsense guide to what the Internet is (and isn't), how it applies to the legal profession, and the different ways it can -- and should -- be used.

The Lawyer's Guide to Marketing on the Internet. This book talks about the pluses and minuses of marketing on the Internet, as well as how to develop an Internet marketing plan.

Leader's Digest: A Review of the Best Books on Leadership. This book will help you find the best books on leadership to help you to achieve extraordinary and exceptional leadership skills.

Leveraging with Legal Assistants. Reviews the changes that have led to increased use of legal assistants and the need to enlarge their role further. Learn specific ways in which a legal assistant can handle a substantial portion of traditional lawyer work.

Microsoft® Word for Windows in One Hour for Lawyers. This book includes special tips for users of Windows 95. It contains four easy lessons--timed at 15 minutes each--that will help lawyers prepare, save, and edit a basic document.

Results-Oriented Financial Management. A Guide to Successful Law Firm Financial Performance. How to manage "the numbers," from setting rates and computing billable hours to calculating net income and preparing the budget. Over 30 charts and statements to help you prepare reports.

Survival Guide for Road Warriors: Essential for the Mobile Lawyer. A guide to using a notebook computer and combinations of equipment and technology so lawyers can be effective in their office, on the road, in the courtroom or at home.

Through the Client's Eyes: New Approaches to Get Clients to Hire You Again and Again. Includes an overview of client relations and sample letters, surveys, and self-assessment questions to gauge your client relations acumen.

TQM in Action: One Firm's Journey Toward Quality and Excellence. A guide to implementing the principles of Total Quality Management in your law firm.

Win-Win Billing Strategies. Represents the first comprehensive analysis of what constitutes "value," and how to bill for it. You'll learn how to initiate and implement different billing methods that make sense for you and your client.

Women Rainmakers' 101+ Best Marketing Tips. A collection of over 130 marketing tips suggested by women rainmakers throughout the country. Includes tips on image, networking, public relations, and advertising.

WordPerfect® 101 for the Law Office. A book for new users of WordPerfect 6.1. It reviews the basics of WordPerfect--creating, editing and saving documents. Includes exercises on diskette.

WordPerfect® 201 for the Law Office. An intermediate course in WordPerfect 6.1. The book delves into advanced editing and automation features. Includes exercises on diskette.

WordPerfect® 6.1 for Windows in One Hour for Lawyers. This is a crash course in the most popular word processing software package used by lawyers. In four lessons, you'll learn the basic steps for getting a simple job done.

WordPerfect® Shortcuts for Lawyers. A fast-track guide to two of WordPerfect's more advanced functions: merge and macros. Includes 4 lessons designed to take 15 minutes each.

Order Form

Qty	Title	LPM Price	Regular Price	Total
______	ABA Guide to Lawyer Trust Accouts (5110374)	$ 69.95	$ 79.95	$________
______	ABA Guide to Legal Marketing (5110341)	69.95	79.95	$________
______	ABA Guide to Prof. Managers in the Law Office (5110373)	69.95	79.95	$________
______	Becoming Computer Literate (5110342)	32.95	39.95	$________
______	Billing Innovations (5110366)	124.95	144.95	$________
______	Changing Jobs, 2nd Ed. (5110334)	49.95	59.95	$________
______	Compensation Plans for Lawyers (5110353)	69.95	79.95	$________
______	Do-It-Yourself Public Relations (5110352)	69.95	79.95	$________
______	Finding the Right Lawyer (5110339)	19.95	19.95	$________
______	Flying Solo, 2nd Ed. (5110328)	59.95	69.95	$________
______	How to Draft Bills Clients Rush to Pay (5110344)	39.95	49.95	$________
______	How to Get and Keep Good Clients (5110347)	99.00	99.00	$________
______	How to Start & Build a Law Practice, 3rd Ed. (5110293)	32.95	39.95	$________
______	Law Office Staff Manual for Solos & Small Firms (5110361)	49.95	59.95	$________
______	Lawyer's Guide to the Internet (5110343)	24.95	29.95	$________
______	Lawyer's Guide to Marketing on the Internet (5110371)	54.95	64.95	$________
______	Leader's Digest (5110356)	49.95	59.95	$________
______	Leveraging with Legal Assistants (5110322)	59.95	69.95	$________
______	Microsoft Word for Windows in One Hour (5110358)	19.95	29.95	$________
______	Results-Oriented Financial Management (5110319)	44.95	54.95	$________
______	Survival Guide for Road Warriors (5110362)	24.95	29.95	$________
______	Through the Client's Eyes (5110337)	69.95	79.95	$________
______	TQM in Action (5110323)	59.95	69.95	$________
______	Win-Win Billing Strategies (5110304)	89.95	99.95	$________
______	Women Rainmakers' 101+ Best Marketing Tips (5110336)	14.95	19.95	$________
______	WordPerfect 101 for the Law Office (5110364)	59.95	64.95	$________
______	WordPerfect 201 for the Law Office (5110365)	59.95	64.95	$________
______	WordPerfect 101 & 201 Package (5110339)	89.90	99.90	$________
______	WordPerfect® 6.1 for Windows in One Hour for Lawyers (5110354)	19.95	29.95	$________
______	WordPerfect® Shortcuts for Lawyers (5110329)	14.95	19.95	$________

***HANDLING**

$ 2.00-$9.99	$2.00
10.00-24.99	$3.95
25.00-49.99	$4.95
50.00 +	$5.95

****TAX**

DC residents add 5.75%
IL residents add 8.75%
MD residents add 5%

SUBTOTAL:	$________
*HANDLING:	$________
**TAX:	$________
TOTAL:	$________

PAYMENT

☐ Check enclosed (Payable to the ABA) ☐ Bill Me

☐ Visa ☐ MasterCard ☐ American Express Account Number:________________ Exp. Date: ________

Signature ________________________________

Name ________________________________

Firm ________________________________

Address ________________________________

City ____________________ State ____________ ZIP ____________

Phone number ________________________________

Mail to: ABA, Publication Orders, P.O. Box 10892, Chicago, IL 60610-0892

Phone: (312) 988-5522 **Fax:** (312) 988-5568

Email: abasvcctr@attmail.com **World WideWeb:** http//www.abanet.org/lpm/catalog

BOOK

THE SECTION OF LAW PRACTICE MANAGEMENT

CUSTOMER COMMENT FORM

ABA

Title of Book: ____________________

We've tried to make this publication as useful, accurate, and readable as possible. Please take 5 minutes to tell us if we succeeded. Your comments and suggestions will help us improve our publications. Thank you!

1. How did you acquire this publication:

☐ by mail order ☐ at a meeting/convention ☐ as a gift

☐ by phone order ☐ at a bookstore ☐ don't know

☐ other: (describe) ____________________

Please rate this publication as follows:

	Excellent	Good	Fair	Poor	Not Applicable
Readability: Was the book easy to read and understand?	☐	☐	☐	☐	☐
Examples/Cases: Were they helpful, practical? Were there enough?	☐	☐	☐	☐	☐
Content: Did the book meet your expectations? Did it cover the subject adequately?	☐	☐	☐	☐	☐
Organization and clarity: Was the sequence of text logical? Was it easy to find what you wanted to know?	☐	☐	☐	☐	☐
Illustrations/forms/checklists: Were they clear and useful? Were there enough?	☐	☐	☐	☐	☐
Physical attractiveness: What did you think of the appearance of the publication (typesetting, printing, etc.)?	☐	☐	☐	☐	☐

Would you recommend this book to another attorney/administrator? ☐ Yes ☐ No

How could this publication be improved? What else would you like to see in it?

____

Do you have other comments or suggestions? ____________________

Name ____________________

Firm/Company ____________________

Address ____________________

City/State/Zip ____________________

Phone ____________________

Firm Size: ____________________ Area of specialization: ____________________

We appreciate your time and help.

Fold

NO POSTAGE
NECESSARY
IF MAILED
IN THE
UNITED STATES

BUSINESS REPLY MAIL

FIRST CLASS PERMIT NO. 16471 CHICAGO, ILLINOIS

POSTAGE WILL BE PAID BY ADDRESSEE

AMERICAN BAR ASSOCIATION
PPM, 8th FLOOR
750 N. LAKE SHORE DRIVE
CHICAGO, ILLINOIS 60611–9851

Fold